Cambridge Elements ☰

Elements in International R

edited by
Jon C. W. Pevehouse
University of Wisconsin-Madison
Tanja A. Börzel
Freie Universität Berlin
Edward D. Mansfield
University of Pennsylvania

CONTESTATIONS OF THE LIBERAL INTERNATIONAL ORDER

A Populist Script of Regional Cooperation

Fredrik Söderbaum
University of Gothenburg

Kilian Spandler
University of Gothenburg

Agnese Pacciardi
Sant'Anna School of Advanced Studies

CAMBRIDGE
UNIVERSITY PRESS

CAMBRIDGE
UNIVERSITY PRESS

University Printing House, Cambridge CB2 8BS, United Kingdom

One Liberty Plaza, 20th Floor, New York, NY 10006, USA

477 Williamstown Road, Port Melbourne, VIC 3207, Australia

314–321, 3rd Floor, Plot 3, Splendor Forum, Jasola District Centre,
New Delhi – 110025, India

79 Anson Road, #06–04/06, Singapore 079906

Cambridge University Press is part of the University of Cambridge.

It furthers the University's mission by disseminating knowledge in the pursuit of
education, learning, and research at the highest international levels of excellence.

www.cambridge.org
Information on this title: www.cambridge.org/9781009015974
DOI: 10.1017/9781009030915

© Fredrik Söderbaum, Kilian Spandler and Agnese Pacciardi 2021

This publication is in copyright. Subject to statutory exception
and to the provisions of relevant collective licensing agreements,
no reproduction of any part may take place without the written
permission of Cambridge University Press.

First published May 2021

A catalogue record for this publication is available from the British Library.

ISBN 978-1-009-01597-4 Paperback
ISSN 2515-706X (online)
ISSN 2515-7302 (print)

Additional resources for this publication at
www.cambridge.org/abstract-contestations-of-the-LIO.

Cambridge University Press has no responsibility for the persistence or accuracy of
URLs for external or third-party internet websites referred to in this publication
and does not guarantee that any content on such websites is, or will remain,
accurate or appropriate.

Contestations of the Liberal International Order

A Populist Script of Regional Cooperation

Elements in International Relations

DOI: 10.1017/9781009030915
First published online: May 2021

Fredrik Söderbaum
University of Gothenburg

Kilian Spandler
University of Gothenburg

Agnese Pacciardi
Sant'Anna School of Advanced Studies

Author for correspondence: Fredrik Söderbaum, fredrik.soderbaum@gu.se

Abstract: A seemingly never-ending stream of observers claims that the populist emphasis on nationalism, identity, and popular sovereignty undermines international collaboration and contributes to the crisis of the Liberal International Order (LIO). Why, then, do populist governments continue to engage in regional and international institutions? This Element unpacks the counter-intuitive inclination towards institutional cooperation in populist foreign policy and discusses its implications for the LIO. Straddling Western and non-Western contexts, it compares the regional cooperation strategies of populist leaders from three continents: Hungarian Prime Minister Viktor Orbán, former Venezuelan President Hugo Chávez, and Philippine President Rodrigo Duterte. The study identifies an emerging populist 'script' of regional cooperation based on notions of popular sovereignty. By embedding regional cooperation in their political strategies, populist leaders are able to contest the LIO and established international organisations without having to revert to unilateral nationalism.

Keywords: global governance, international organisation, nationalism, populism, regional organisation

© Fredrik Söderbaum, Kilian Spandler, and Agnese Pacciardi 2021

ISBNs: 9781009015974 (PB), 9781009030915 (OC)
ISSNs: 2515-706X (online), 2515-7302 (print)

Contents

1 Introduction

A seemingly never-ending stream of observers warns that the global rise of populism may result in overt nationalist unilateralism and the demise of the Liberal International Order (LIO) undergirding world politics since the end of World War II (Colgan & Keohane, 2017; De Spiegeleire et al., 2017; Ikenberry, 2011, 2018a; Slaughter, 2017; Zakaria, 2016). Indeed, US President Donald Trump's 'America First' slogan and the vagaries of Brexit point towards institutional disengagement and foreign policies defined in line with more narrow nationalist self-interests. From this perspective, the upsurge in populism in many Western and non-Western states poses an existential threat to the LIO.

Common definitions of the LIO describe it as a Western-centric set of formal and informal norms and institutions promoting ideas of political liberalism (democratic values and human rights), economic liberalism (open markets and neoliberal policies), and liberal internationalism (principled multilateralism and institutionalised cooperation) (Börzel & Risse, 2019; Kreuder-Sonnen & Rittberger, 2020: 5). Most contemporary populist movements are clearly at odds with these ideas, as they reject universalist and pluralist social values, thrive on nationalist ideology, and are protective of state sovereignty (Orellana & Michelsen, 2019). This sense of incompatibility between populism and the LIO is reinforced by interpretations that see populism as a backlash against forces of globalisation and liberal democratic values, as well as by the fact that its proponents often contest and critique established global and regional norms and institutions (Chryssogelos, 2017; Halikiopoulou et al., 2012; Verbeek & Zaslove, 2017; Zürn, 2004).

Most assessments of populist responses to the LIO focus on what populist movements claim to be *against,* rather than the kinds of foreign policies their leaders actually deploy once in power. One could argue, of course, that this is what populism is all about: it thrives on rejecting the established order, rather than providing a positive and clearly defined countervision. However, recent studies show that populist governments around the world frequently engage in various sorts of international cooperation, not least on a regional scale (Burrier, 2019; Copelovitch & Pevehouse, 2019; Destradi & Plagemann, 2019; Riggirozzi & Tussie, 2012; Verbeek & Zaslove, 2017; Wajner, 2019). In Europe, many populist-nationalist parties are sceptical of the European Union (EU) but nevertheless support European cooperation and integration (De Spiegeleire et al., 2017: vi). In some instances, populists have even created regional institutions of their own, such as the Visegrád Group (V4) of Central and Eastern European states and the Bolivarian Alliance for the Peoples of Our America (ALBA).

This Element is motivated by the failure of existing literature on the contestation of the LIO to reconcile the engagement of a significant number of populist governments in international and regional cooperation with their image as nationalists, sovereigntists, and unilateralists. A main reason for the conspicuous silence on this subject is that analyses from within the discipline of International Relations have focused on state positions or institutional characteristics as drivers of contestation, while neglecting domestic politics (Börzel & Zürn, 2021; see also Acharya, 2018; Slaughter, 2017). For instance, power-transition theories explain the crisis of the LIO as a result of waning US hegemony and the increasing strength of emerging powers in the international system (Kagan, 2017; Kupchan, 2012; Layne, 2012; Mearsheimer, 2001). For rational institutionalists, the resilience of the LIO depends on whether emerging powers view international institutions as effective instruments for addressing policy challenges (Ikenberry, 2011, 2018b). Sociological institutionalists focus on the ideational appeal of the norms and rules of the LIO, and the degree to which potential challengers are socialised into accepting them as the 'rules of the game' (Johnston, 2008; Kent, 2002; Li, 2012). International political economists, meanwhile, emphasise that rising inequalities and exclusions between and within societies create resistance from those who perceive themselves as losing out under globalisation (Colgan & Keohane, 2017; see also Hooghe et al., 2019: 736–7). Finally, authors concerned with international authority see contestation as a political backlash against the growing intrusion of international institutions into affairs that had hitherto been considered prerogatives of nation-states (Börzel & Zürn, 2021; Kreuder-Sonnen & Rittberger, 2020; Zürn, 2004).

These approaches explain contestation of the LIO either as a consequence of institutional qualities and performance (Kreuder-Sonnen & Rittberger, 2020; Tallberg & Zürn, 2019) or as a function of states' (or other actors') positions in relation to international institutions. Börzel and Zürn (2021), for example, argue that 'it is the position of contestants towards liberal authority and their position in the contested institution that *pre-determine* the strategy of contestation' (emphasis added). We agree, of course, that actors' differential exposure to the power effects of the LIO inevitably shapes their opinions on it, as well as their contestation strategies – but only to a certain extent. By focusing too heavily on international explanatory variables as drivers of contestation, existing accounts leave a number of questions unaddressed. First, states with similar structural positions in the global system contest the LIO to very different degrees and in different ways (think of France under Macron vs Brexit-era Britain). Second, the stance of states towards the LIO can also drastically change despite stability in their positions (think of the United States under Obama vs Trump). Finally, there are several common traits in the ways in which states that have very different positions within the global system contest the LIO. For example, this Element identifies remarkable commonalities in the way populist leaders in Hungary, Venezuela, and the Philippines have contested the LIO, even though the first is a member of the Organisation for Economic Co-operation and Development (OECD), the second has for a long time been ostracised by the dominating members of the LIO, and the third is considered a developing country.

On the basis of these observations, we contend that contestation is not reducible to actors' positions in the international system but depends heavily on domestic politics. Unless the black box of the state is unpacked, we will fail to understand how internal political mechanisms shape contestation at the international level. This Element therefore follows the suggestion by Hooghe et al. (2019) to bring domestic politics into the debate about the LIO. A core assumption – seemingly obvious but often neglected in International Relations literature – is that the foreign policy positions of state leaders are shaped by their domestic political strategies. This may seem self-evident but, as we just argued, it is often overlooked in scholarship on the contestation of the LIO. All politicians base their claims to power on certain representations of 'the political' – that is, they give different answers to questions such as the following: 'Who are the main groups in society?' 'What are they fighting over?' and 'How should conflicts between them be solved?' (Laclau & Mouffe, 2001). They thus define what is at stake in the political game and position themselves in a way that is supposed to mobilise and maintain political support. The strategies of populist leaders are different from those of politicians running on liberal pluralistic platforms but also from those pursuing, say, a fascist model of political mobilisation. We argue that these domestic political strategies of populist leaders translate into specific framings and institutional preferences regarding international cooperation in the leaders' foreign policies. Analysing them allows us to draw a more comprehensive and nuanced picture of how they contest the LIO and what alternatives they offer.

Our main argument is that many populist leaders are *not* anti-internationalist but in fact ascribe a positive value to *certain forms* of international cooperation, especially regional mechanisms that are malleable to populist ideas and preferences. Grounded in theoretical scholarship on populism, we develop a framework that identifies three populist framings of regional cooperation: anti-liberalism, multilayered and threatened identity, and popular sovereignty. Just like all heads of state and government, populist leaders endorse forms of cooperation that further their political agendas. Framing regionalism according to populist strategy predisposes them towards three core institutional preferences: leader-driven formats, political symbolism, and *à la carte* cooperation.

To substantiate our argument, we compare speech acts on regional cooperation by populist leaders from three continents: Hungarian Prime Minister Viktor Orbán, former Venezuelan President Hugo Chávez, and Philippine President Rodrigo Duterte. While these three leaders represent different guises of populism regarding geographical location and ideological proclivities, they show clear commonalities in their framing of regional cooperation and their institutional preferences. We therefore contend that there is an emerging populist 'script' of regional cooperation – made up of the various frames and institutional preferences outlined earlier – that populists draw on in their contestation of the LIO. The notion of a 'script' is inspired by research in the Berlin-based Cluster of Excellence 'Contestations of the Liberal Script', where it broadly denotes a set of ideas about political and social order (Börzel & Zürn, 2021). We use the term here in a somewhat narrower sense, where it refers to a narrative that contextualises foreign policy positions and decisions in ideas about the legitimacy of the existing international order. From this perspective, populist leaders' framings and the formation and projection of institutional preferences regarding regional cooperation form part of broader strategies of delegitimating the LIO and legitimating alternative visions for international order.

The Element is structured as follows. Section 2 reviews the emerging International Relations literature on the international dimension of populism. These works provide theoretical and empirical support for the argument that – contrary to a simplified association of populism with unilateral nationalism – some elements of populist politics have a transboundary dimension. Section 3 teases out the implications of these insights for the regional level. Grounded in theories of populism, it argues that populist leaders and governments derive their institutional preferences from specific framings that relate regional cooperation to their domestic political strategies. Sections 4, 5, and 6 present our analysis of the three populist leaders' speech acts on regional cooperation. The three case studies draw on official statements, interviews, and press releases during the period of incumbency of each of the three leaders. The similarities in framings and institutional preferences, which are summarised in Section 7, suggest that the logic of populist politics incentivises populist leaders to adopt strategies of regional cooperation that contest certain aspects of the LIO. We discuss the implications of these findings for broader research on the contestation of the LIO in Section 8. The concluding Section 9 argues that the rise of populists to power around the world does not herald the end of international cooperation but presages specific forms of regional cooperation, namely, those that enhance popular sovereignty, boost the status of national leaders, and advance domestic populist strategies.

2 The International Dimension of Populism

Most scholars of populism agree that an antagonistic logic of pitting 'the elite' against 'the people' is at the core of populist politics (Canovan, 1999; Meny & Surel, 2002; Mudde, 2004; Taggart, 2000). Scholars approaching the phenomenon from the perspective of comparative politics or political theory usually assume that the notion of 'the people' is constructed on the basis of nationalist (or ethnic) identities. Imaginations of the people invoke the idea of a 'homogeneous' (Mudde, 2004: 543) or 'monolithic' (Taggart, 2000: 92) community belonging to a common 'heartland' that often has nationalistic connotations (Taggart, 2004: 274). Meanwhile, incumbent governments, often in alliance with powerful actors in the national economies of nation-states, represent the elite. As a consequence, populism has primarily been studied as a national phenomenon (Mudde & Rovira Kaltwasser, 2013). Paul Taggart (2000: 96), one of the field's main proponents, expressed this intuitive association: 'Internationalism and cosmopolitanism are anathema to populists.' The attitude towards those concerns outside the boundaries of the populists' chosen people is diffident. Isolationism and insularity are the natural predispositions of populists.

By contrast, recent International Relations scholarship has emphasised that dynamics beyond national boundaries clearly influence domestic populist politics and vice versa (Chryssogelos, 2014; Verbeek & Zaslove, 2019: 12–14). Empirically, populist governments do engage in various forms of international cooperation (Copelovitch & Pevehouse, 2019; Verbeek & Zaslove, 2017). These works demonstrate that even though we observe an obvious affinity to nationalist ideology among many contemporary populist movements, nationalism needs to be conceptually separated from populism (see also Bonikowski et al., 2019; De Cleen, 2017; De Cleen & Stavrakakis, 2017; De Spiegeleire et al., 2017: 37–8).

On the basis of these insights, researchers have started to unpack the nexus between the domestic and the international dimensions of populism (Chryssogelos, 2017; Stengel et al., 2019). Studies of global governance have for a long time claimed that the hollowing out of national democracy by international organisations or regional integration has caused a populist backlash (Mair, 2009; Zürn, 2004). A main entry point for theorising this argument was offered by Laclau (2005), who argued that the people–elite antagonism was discursively constructed in political struggles. This means that neither group is necessarily confined to national boundaries. Building on these thoughts, International Relations scholars have pointed out that the elite may take on a transnational dimension (Copelovitch & Pevehouse, 2019; Holliday, 2019). Especially when populists assume power domestically, they may frame their interests against the outside world, not least against established multilateral and regional institutions such as the European Union (EU), the North Atlantic Treaty Organization (NATO), or the World Trade Organization (WTO) (Chryssogelos, 2017). On the other side of the antagonism, as Chryssogelos (2017: 2) points out, populism does not necessarily depend on a national definition of the people:

> The 'people' for whom populists speak in international affairs can very well transcend national borders, as evidenced, for example, in the foreign policies of Hugo Chavez [sic] and Mahmud Ahmadinejad, who aimed to represent trans-national constituencies like the Global South, the Islamic world, the world poor, etc.

Such transnational notions of 'the people' open additional ways in which populism may acquire an international dimension (De Cleen et al., 2019; Miller-Idriss, 2019; Moffitt, 2017; Zeeman, 2019). Not only do many populists construct the people and the elite in ways that transcend national borders, they may also favour international cooperation by virtue of a sense of common identity or a strategic opposition to a common enemy (Verbeek & Zaslove, 2017). Needless to say, the international/transnational dimension of populism does not present itself in the same way across time and space. For example, in Europe, the end of the Cold War, globalisation, and the EU's integration processes acted as decisive drivers of populism. In Latin America, populism cannot be understood without taking into account the impact of colonial history and the economic transformations in the twentieth century (Verbeek & Zaslove, 2017). Populists can draw on such historical and regional contexts to reinforce their support by translating them into domestic and foreign policy strategies and discourses (Hadiz & Chryssogelos, 2017).

Furthermore, whether and how populists engage at the international level depend on their broader political dispositions (Verbeek & Zaslove, 2017). Mudde (2004) has prominently conceptualised populism as a 'thin-centred' ideology around which actors can reconstruct a variety of more comprehensive and complex political world views (see also Taggart, 2000). Most frequently, authors distinguish between left-wing and right-wing (De Cleen, 2017), redistributionist and nativist (Copelovitch & Pevehouse, 2019), or inclusive and exclusive populism (Mudde & Rovira Kaltwasser, 2013). Although both left-wing and right-wing populists rely on the opposition between the people and elites, the people–elite antagonism plays out differently for left-wing and right-wing populists, because only the latter develop their anti-elitism alongside a nativist ideology (Copelovitch & Pevehouse, 2019). Hence, the critique of left-wing and right-wing populists may target different aspects of the LIO.

For example, Copelovitch and Pevehouse (2019) expect that nationalist (or nativist) populists will cooperate when it makes their state stronger vis-à-vis other states even if they have little interest in the mutual gains of international cooperation. Destradi and Plagemann (2019: 13) substantiate this with their analysis of the populist-nationalist Modi government in India, which positioned itself as a facilitator in multilateral agreements (such as the Paris Agreement) to promote the image of India as a global citizen and partner in multilateral and regional institutions. Left-wing or redistributionist populists, meanwhile, should be open to international cooperation as long as it is unlikely to exacerbate wealth inequalities. The various regional cooperation projects launched by Latin American leaders during the so-called 'Pink Tide' of left-wing populism are cases in point (Wajner, 2019).

Previous research thus provides theoretical and empirical support for the hypothesis that populists are not principally opposed to international cooperation. However, most scholars have almost exclusively fixated on certain particularities of populist foreign policy in different parts of the world. Even where comparative perspectives are adopted, this is often for the sake of teasing out differences between 'thick' variants of populism, not asking about common trends and approaches (Destradi & Plagemann, 2019). The idiographic orientation of existing scholarship has prevented generalisation and theory building about cooperation among populist governments as well as the formation of empirical knowledge about how populists contest the LIO and whether populist leaders are formulating coherent alternative conceptions of international order.

One aspect that has remained puzzling from a theoretical point of view is populist leaders' apparent preference for cooperation on a regional scale. Existing theories of regionalism offer few insights on this issue. In fact, most conventional approaches implicitly or explicitly assume that there is an inherent competition between populism (at least in its right-wing form) and regionalism (Hooghe & Marks, 2009). These approaches are typically rooted in Western understandings of regionalism, according to which integration and cooperation follow a liberal script that aims to provide effective governance on issues such as trade, security, human rights, and so on (Börzel & Van Hüllen, 2015; Jupille et al., 2013; Risse, 2016). From this perspective, the main hallmark of regionalism is the transfer of national sovereignty to regional institutions for the purpose of providing public goods. Since the nationalist orientation of populist regimes often opposes such transfers (Copelovitch & Pevehouse, 2019), populism seems ultimately irreconcilable with the liberal script of regionalism.

Alternative approaches that aim at redressing the liberal bias of existing scholarship have done little to address this gap. During the past decade, the sharp increase in research on the 'dark sides' of regionalism and 'authoritarian regionalism' has stimulated a range of new insights about when, why, and how regionalism is used by political leaders and governments for regime survival, regime boosting, and legitimacy boosting or as a smokescreen for achieving narrow interests (Debre & Morgenbesser, 2017; Kneuer et al., 2019; Kreuder-Sonnen, 2018; Obydenkova & Libman, 2019; Russo & Stoddard, 2018; Söderbaum, 2016). Even though this literature details how authoritarian leaders use regionalism to challenge liberal-functional principles and the LIO more broadly, it offers surprisingly few insights into how populism shapes regional and global governance in today's world. We suspect that one reason for this is conceptual uncertainty about how authoritarianism relates to populism – an issue on which we briefly elaborate in the next section.

Overall, the comprehensive implications of the rise of populism for the LIO remain hard to gauge. Accordingly, the following section develops a comparative framework that grounds populist strategies of regional cooperation in the antagonism between the people and the elite that forms populism's core political logic. Such a framework allows us to formulate expectations about the framings and institutional preferences through which populist leaders embed regional cooperation in their domestic politics; these expectations will then be checked against empirical realities through the three case studies of Victor Orbán, Hugo Chávez, and Rodrigo Duterte.

3 Framework

'Populism' is a notoriously contested concept, and critics have pointed out that ongoing debates have suffered from its being used as a buzzword without clear definitions (Stengel, 2019). There is also a tendency to conflate populism with nationalism and authoritarianism (Bonikowski, 2017). As a result, too many observers treat current contestations of the LIO as much more homogeneous than they actually are, without asking who contests what and on what grounds. In a situation where an ever-increasing number of regimes and political leaders are labelled populist, it is necessary to uphold certain distinctions and not lump everyone who is not 'liberal' into one category. To provide some conceptual clarity, Section 3.1 situates our own stance in relation to existing theoretical approaches to populism. We side with those scholars who treat it first and foremost as a political strategy. Based on this perspective, Section 3.2 presents a framework that allows us to analyse how populist leaders integrate ideas about regional cooperation into their political strategies. Our conceptualisation consists of two core elements – *framings* and *institutional preferences* – which allow an exploration of how leaders represent regional cooperation both in their speech acts and in their strategic considerations regarding the institutional forms such cooperation takes. Finally, Section 3.3 presents the research design and methodological approach of the study.

3.1 Research Approach and Conceptualisation

A range of different approaches can be applied to populism. Some focus on the distinctive features of the political movements that drive populist politics (Di Tella, 1965). Others define populism as an ideology (Canovan, 2002; Mudde, 2004) or a discourse (Aslanidis, 2016; Laclau, 2005). More recently, Benjamin Moffit (2016) has explored the characteristics of populism as a specific style of doing politics. Our own exploration of populist approaches is grounded in Kurt Weyland's work on populism as a political strategy (Weyland, 2001, 2017; see also Miller-Idriss, 2019). More specifically, we define populism as a strategy for maintaining governmental power – that is, we do not focus on the initial mobilisation of opposition to ruling parties but on how leaders sustain popular support once they have attained office. At its core, this strategy relies on speech acts that construct the 'morally pure people' and the corrupt elite as antagonistic group identities (Bonikowski, 2017: 186). Populist leaders then legitimate themselves as the exclusive representatives of the people versus the elite.

Arguing over whether populism is an ideology, a discourse, or a strategy may seem like ontological nitpicking, and our framework does indeed borrow substantial insights about how populist logics play into regional strategies from scholars who adhere to different schools. However, taking a strategic approach offers several analytical advantages for the purpose of our study. For instance, taking a top-down point of view focusing on political leaders and the ways in which they attempt to mobilise and maintain support provides us with a more immediate point of access to our research problem. Bottom-up perspectives of sociopolitical, ideological, and discursive approaches are certainly not irrelevant for a study of populists in power, as they may shed light on the broader societal support structures for their leadership. We argue, though, that it is the political strategy undergirding that leadership that ultimately tells us how they contest the LIO.

Defining populism as a political strategy helps us disentangle it from related concepts and thus avoid several confusions arising in previous debates. First, our approach provides a conceptual grounding for anyone who seeks to avoid the fallacy of equating populism with nationalism or nationalist foreign policies. Seeing populism as a strategy is not at odds with the argument from the ideological strand of the literature that populism's political logic is compatible with different political world views (Bonikowski, 2017: 186–7). Leaders who mobilise support by pitting the people against the elite may strategically pick and choose between broader political programmes to contextualise and legitimate their rhetorical claims. Nationalism as an exclusionary identity of belonging, then, is merely one of such programmes (Miller-Idriss, 2019: 20; Weyland, 2017: 55–64). While most populist leaders tap into some form of nationalist rhetoric, their stances on regional cooperation are often also shaped by other ideological bases, such as socialism, pan-regionalism, or religious conservatism.[1] These doctrines have different effects on how foreign policy and regional cooperation are framed. This helps us understand some of the complexities of populist ideas about regional cooperation – for example, the parallel invocation of national and regional identities.

Second, a strategic approach helps us clarify the relation between populism and authoritarianism. Whereas populism as a political strategy ultimately aims at legitimation – that is, mobilising and maintaining voluntary support among political followers – authoritarianism is a mode of governing based on non-pluralistic institutions and practices aimed at centralising authority and stymying the kinds of political competition encouraged by liberal democracies (Bonikowski, 2017: 189–91). It can therefore also contain more directly restraining and coercive means of securing power. Of course, populism and authoritarianism can be mutually reinforcing, and some authors argue that populism has a natural tendency towards authoritarian modes of governing (Müller, 2016: 44–9). Others, however, maintain that it may also support democratisation (Mudde & Rovira Kaltwasser, 2017: 86–93; Stengel, 2019). While the relationship between populism and authoritarianism is an important debate, it stretches beyond the purposes of this Element, and we merely take the contention over the issue as a further indication that the two concepts should remain separated.

Keeping populism as a political strategy distinct from both nationalism as an ideology and authoritarianism as an institutional mode of governing prevents us from falsely ascribing elements of the contestation of the LIO (such as unilateralism) to populist tendencies. There are nationalist foreign policies that have little to do with populism. For example, nationalist governments relying primarily on patronage networks are more likely to seek partnerships with international donors who allow them to extract the kinds of resources needed to maintain patron–client relations, rather than with like-minded governments. The central role of hierarchical institutions and militarisation in authoritarian regimes, meanwhile, may create a tendency to develop an offensive militaristic foreign policy outlook. None of these tendencies is reducible to populism,

---

[1] These conceptual differences are also emphasised by Mudde and Rovira Kaltwasser (2017: 8) and Weyland (2017: 55–64).

which – as our study shows – in fact encourages a cooperative foreign policy outlook that appears at odds with purely nationalist or authoritarian tendencies.

To get to the core of how regional cooperation fits into the strategies of populist leaders, we follow Chryssogelos's (2010, 2017) argument that the domestic logic of populist politics translates into certain dispositions regarding foreign policy. In line with this 'second image' approach, we analyse populist strategies of regional cooperation on two levels: frames and institutional preferences. In the social sciences, *frames* are commonly defined as schemata of representation through which actors – in our case, the leaders of populist governments – organise reality in ways that connect it to existing knowledge, ideologies, and normative dispositions (Entman, 1993; Goffman, 1974). Several authors have argued that framing is part of the rhetorical strategies through which populists mobilise support (Miller-Idriss, 2019: 18; see also Aslanidis, 2016: 99). Accordingly, we argue that leaders frame regional cooperation in a way that relates it to their broader political agendas by interpreting it through the logic of the antagonism between the people and the elite.

Beyond simply representing reality, frames define problems, diagnose causes, enable moral judgements, prescribe solutions, and motivate action (Benford & Snow, 2000: 615–18; Entman, 1993: 52). In performing these functions, they privilege certain interpretations of problems and highlight potential solutions while excluding alternative points of view, thus shaping dispositions for action. It has been argued that exposure to populist framings increases voters' preferences for populist parties (Hameleers et al., 2018), but the argument can be extended to leaders' foreign policy strategies. Frames shape the policy preferences and choices of international actors (Lenz, 2018: 41), and we argue that populist framings of regional cooperation predispose leaders to view certain institutional forms as more favourable than others. At the same time, framing can legitimate actions: once leaders have made certain institutional choices, frames can justify and 'sell' these decisions to their key audiences as part of their broader political quest. In sum, while frames do not determine specific preferences in a strictly causal sense, they do constitute the dispositional context within which populists formulate their concrete preferences regarding institutional cooperation.

While the frames and preferences we identify derive in the first instance from the logic of domestic populist politics, we must also assume that ideas about regional cooperation diffuse among populist governments. As we noted in Section 1, scholars have attributed the long-lasting hegemony of the LIO to the spread of a 'liberal script' (Börzel & Zürn, 2021). In a deliberate analogy, we contend that the frames and institutional preferences presented next have come to form a broadly available populist script of regional cooperation, which leaders adopting populist strategies can draw on to contest the LIO.

3.2 Populist Framings of Regional Cooperation

A growing literature shows that populist leaders are not principally opposed to international collaboration and that they do in fact engage in various international collaborative projects, especially at the regional level. Drawing on previous research on populism, especially those works that seek to explore the people–elite antagonism as populism's core political logic, we contend that populist leaders use three main frames to represent and justify their foreign policies in regard to regional cooperation: (i) anti-liberalism, (ii) multiple and threatened identity, and (iii) popular sovereignty.

Anti-Liberalism. 'Liberalism' serves as a frequently employed code – or, in Laclau's (2005) terms, a floating signifier – for populists' construction of the *Other* that deprives the 'ordinary people' of what is rightfully theirs (Canovan, 1999: 19; Galston, 2018). This is especially true beyond the nation-state, where anti-liberalism provides grounds for rejecting what populists perceive as a hegemonic approach to domestic and international 'good' governance advanced primarily by Western states and liberal elites (Börzel & Zürn, 2021; Chryssogelos, 2010). Through inter- and supranational institutions, these elites are said to act *against* the interests of the people (Miller-Idriss, 2019: 25; Mudde & Rovira Kaltwasser, 2017: 35). Accordingly, populists frame regional cooperation in a way that contests the liberal script of regionalism, even if the precise content of populist criticism often remains vague and varies according to different ideological leanings (Destradi & Plagemann, 2019: 3–4). For example, some populists promote free trade, while others oppose it (De Spiegeleire, 2017 et al.: 80–2). At the same time, populists endorse regional cooperation if it represents counterhegemonic or defensive projects, sometimes even within the framework of broader projects such as the EU (Legler, 2010a, 2010b; Riggirozzi, 2012). This may explain why regional or mega-regional populist projects gain more traction than multilateral ones.

Multiple and Threatened Identity. Populism legitimates itself by reference to the people as an 'imagined community' (Anderson, 1991). Through mythical narratives of virtue and authenticity, the people are constructed as the constituency of all populist politics (Canovan, 2002; Meny & Surel, 2002). They are imagined as a community threatened in their integrity or even existence, 'held back by the collusion of foreign forces and self-serving elites at home' (Colgan & Keohane, 2017: 36). The frequent emphasis on constructions of people as a 'homogeneous' (Mudde, 2004: 543) or 'monolithic' (Taggart, 2000: 92) community in the literature obscures the fact that such identities may in fact be multilayered. Of course, if wedded to a right-wing, nationalist 'thick' ideology, populist identity constructions will take on exclusionary forms (Bonikowski, 2017: 184–5; Miller-Idriss, 2019: 21). However, Sutherland (2005: 143) points out that national identity is just 'one of multiple identities capable of commanding loyalty and legitimacy in the political arena . . . regional identity can either clash or co-exist with national belonging, and this relationship is ideologically determined' (see also Herrmann et al., 2004; Hooghe & Marks, 2009). Populists politicise identity but do not necessarily perceive regional and national belonging as a zero-sum game (Checkel & Katzenstein, 2009). Strategically invoking transnational bonds may help reinforce the people–elite antagonism – for example, by summoning solidarity against a common enemy. On a regional level, contextual patterns like common history, ethnic bonds, and cultural or religious ties can provide resources for such constructions of transnational identity that may not be readily available on the level of a global community (Herrmann et al., 2004). Thus, what makes populist identities distinct from, say, cosmopolitan ones is not their (national) scale or homogeneity but the imaginary of a community under threat from a corrupt elite as the defining Other. Regional cooperation can appear as a way of collectively defending the integrity of these identities.[2] This explains why regional identity may sometimes be an ideological tool that populist governments use 'to maintain the central importance of the national construct within regional projects' (Sutherland, 2005: 143).

Popular sovereignty.   The populist logic draws on the notion of a virtuous majority that has been disenfranchised by a detached and corrupt minority (Taggart, 2000). According to Mudde (2004: 543), populist ideology 'argues that politics should be an expression of the *volonté générale* (general will) of the people'. By consequence, the notion of popular sovereignty and the leader's role in 'taking back control' for the voiceless by circumventing established representative institutions is essential in populist politics (Canovan, 2002; Laclau, 2005; Meny & Surel, 2002). Beyond the state, this translates into narratives that see popular sovereignty as threatened by the LIO, which encourages the delegation of authority and external intervention and thus exacerbates the people's loss of autonomy (De Spiegeleire et al., 2017: 76–8). In contrast to narrowly nationalist foreign policy, populist

---

[2]   The notion of a threat to the integrity of the people as a mobilising moment is emphasised, for example, in Taggart's (2000) characterisation of populism as relying on a sense of crisis that calls for the defence of the 'heartland'.

foreign policy is at its core not about promoting the nation but about re-establishing an ostensibly lost popular sovereignty (see Verbeek & Zaslove, 2017; Zürn, 2004). Chryssogelos (2017: 2) goes as far as to say that 'whether defined along national, regional or transnational lines, "sovereignty" is probably the term that most accurately captures the populist logic of international affairs.' Accordingly, populist leaders endorse forms of regional cooperation that are compatible with particular notions of sovereignty. Rather than challenging the state, regionalism is supposed to safeguard or even enhance the leader's role in taking back control from the elite and giving it to the people. In Legler's (2013: 334–5) terms, 'national sovereignty is interwoven with and mutually reinforced by regional sovereignty.' Framing regional cooperation in terms of popular sovereignty thus ties it back to the people as an imagined constituency and the only legitimate source of sovereignty.

3.3 Institutional Preferences for Regional Cooperation

We expect populist leaders to endorse specific types of cooperation that are compatible with the diagnostic, prescriptive, and motivational implications of the way in which they frame regionalism. Three core institutional preferences can be derived from previous theoretical work: (i) leader-driven formats, (ii) symbolism, and (iii) *à la carte* cooperation.

Leader-Driven Formats.   Populists strongly prefer cooperation formats that are dominated by heads of state and governments. Theories of populism have frequently emphasised its predisposition towards personalistic leadership, where the leader is seen as the representative of the people who will take back control from the conspiring elite (Moffitt, 2016; Taggart, 2000). Several authors have argued that populist leaders rely on plebiscitarian legitimation (e.g. Barr, 2009; Weyland, 2017). This form of leadership rejects institutional representation and bureaucratic authority in favour of an (imagined) direct link between the leader and the constituency (Weyland, 2001: 14). According to Taggart (2000: 101–2), 'It is their rejection of the institutionalization inherent in representative politics that leads populists to mobilize, and so if they can do this in a way that avoids complex institutional structures then this suits them.' On the regional level, populists consequently oppose the liberal script of transferring sovereignty to regional organisations through delegation and pooling, as such transfers would amount to (further) ceding of control from the people to the elite (see De Spiegeleire et al., 2017: 75). Instead, they prefer intergovernmental designs that emphasise member-state autonomy and high-level interaction, because such approaches accord populists their role as the defenders of popular sovereignty (see Destradi & Plagemann, 2019: 14–17). They may also engage in 'forum shopping', whereby governments scale their engagement with specific regional initiatives up or down, or even create new ones, depending on where they think they can best project their leadership role.

Symbolism. Populists prefer regional forms of cooperation that provide space for symbolic acts through which the people–elite antagonism is enacted on the regional political plain. Moffit (2016) describes populism first and foremost as a performative political style, in which the leader appears as the performer and the people as the audience. The goal of populist performance is to continually reproduce the identity of the people and to legitimate the leader as someone who represents the people and who is distinct from the elite. While popular demands can be mobilised for these enactments, the actual solution of such demands is secondary, if not elusive (Laclau, 2005). Populists thus strive to instrumentalise regional cooperation as an additional stage on which popular representation and anti-elitism can be enacted before a domestic and international audience. In addition, populist regimes can mutually legitimate one another in regional events through symbolic acts. Consequently, populists prefer forms of cooperation that offer space for symbolic politics that buttress domestic support over those that are concerned with technical and administrative work on policy problems. Policy development and implementation are de-emphasised.

À la Carte **Cooperation.** At its core, populist leadership is not ideologically motivated but opportunistically oriented towards the maintenance of power. As Weyland (2017: 60) puts it, 'populist leaders like undertaking new initiatives, often with great fanfare; but thorough program elaboration and careful, systematic implementation are often missing.' Populists therefore prefer regional cooperation that is *à la carte* in terms of policy areas. While regional cooperation may cover a broad range of fields on paper, populist leaders eventually choose to follow through only on those fields of cooperation that reinforce their domestic political strategies. Although populists may seek effective cooperation on these issues, such cooperation is not primarily oriented towards providing public goods or pursuing broader milieu goals (Chryssogelos, 2017). Instead, the preference for problem-solving cooperation in specific areas is strategic and instrumental. For example, it might enable rent-seeking for the leader and the ruling elite or provide symbolic resources in legitimation strategies 'at home'. In relation to the latter, Destradi and Plagemann (2019: 7) argue that populists are likely to politicise selected international issues for the purpose of domestic mobilisation because of their constant need to performatively enact abroad their self-proclaimed identity as representatives of the people. This resonates with the argument from domestic populism research that populists politicise certain key demands through which people express grievances and dissatisfaction with established political institutions (Laclau, 2005: 73–4; Meny & Surel, 2002: 13–14). The opportunism of populist strategy also encourages forum shopping to realise short-term goals (see Wajner & Roniger, 2019: 7–8). Indeed, recent scholarship shows that when participating in international cooperation, populists seem to cherry-pick international commitments that suit their purposes (De Spiegeleire et al., 2017: 99). On the regional level, Dabène (2012: 62) observes a trend of integration *à la carte,* in which a variety of flexible regional and subregional arrangements make it possible for member-states to adapt their level of commitment selectively to individual schemes according to their preferences. This selective approach provides an additional rationale for forum shopping besides the desire to project a leadership role in regional cooperation. We expect populist leaders to endorse regional cooperation because it helps them strategically tailor their government's international engagement according to the needs of their domestic agenda – for example, by securing transfer payments in sectors that are sensitive for the national economy, by showcasing geopolitical alliance building against an antagonist, or by performing policies that symbolically defend the integrity of the people.

What is particular to populist leaders is not that they make strategic decisions about whether or not to engage in regional cooperation. Quite like their populist counterparts, liberal and functionally oriented governments weigh cooperation gains against the 'sovereignty costs' they expect to pay – that is, the constraints on national decision-making that go along with joining international institutions (see Hafner-Burton et al., 2015; Moravcsik, 1998). What is unique for populist leaders is that the logic of their political strategies leads them to adopt a conception of cooperation gains and sovereignty costs that diverges significantly from that of both liberal and authoritarian leaders. As liberal intergovernmentalism argues, liberals are primarily interested in functional cooperation gains, such as transboundary problem-solving, that satisfy the demands of domestic interest groups (Moravcsik, 1997). The emerging literature on authoritarian regionalism shows that authoritarian leaders mainly engage in cooperation with a view to hard-core regime security, in the sense of mutual assistance in suppressing domestic opposition and external intervention (Obydenkova & Libman, 2019). For populist leaders, the gains are of a more performative nature. Cooperation is desirable insofar as it enables them to portray themselves as representatives of popular sovereignty and thus enhance their domestic self-legitimation. Functional cooperation gains and the achievement of public goods are not the main determinants in this calculation but are only relevant insofar as they can be sold to domestic constituencies as steps towards strengthening popular sovereignty and taking back control as defined in populist political strategies. The examples for *à la carte* regionalism in the empirical Sections 4–6 include several cases where such calculations become obvious, such as Hugo Chávez's role in devising development cooperation programmes in ALBA and the Southern Common Market (Mercosur) to benefit the poor, or the V4 states' ambition to play a leading role in the EU's Common Security and Defence Policy.

3.4 Methodology

To illustrate how frames and institutional preferences shape populist approaches to regional cooperation, the following three sections present comparative case studies of populist leaders' discourses on regional cooperation in three countries; the leaders studied are Hungarian Prime Minister Viktor Orbán, former Venezuelan President Hugo Chávez, and Philippine President Rodrigo Duterte. While there is an emerging literature on the foreign policy preferences of populist leaders, to our knowledge the study represents the most systematic attempt to date to analyse the behaviour of populist leaders vis-à-vis regional and international organisations.

The rationale behind the case selection was to identify important similarities across a set of diverse and substantively important cases, which would lend methodological credibility to the broad claim made regarding the emergence of a populist script. More specifically, our cases have been selected to combine variation regarding ideological orientation and geographical location with a relevance for the study of regional cooperation. First, while all three leaders have been described as relying heavily on populist strategies – including in their foreign policies – they are associated with different political projects and ideological commitments. Orbán's nativist and authoritarian leanings make him an exponent of Europe's current wave of far-right populism (Plattner, 2019). Chávez is arguably the icon of Latin America's 'Pink Tide' of populism, with strong socialist overtones (Chodor & McCarthy-Jones, 2013). Meanwhile, Duterte has been associated with an authoritarian but somewhat ideologically flexible form of populism that is often seen as a specifically Southeast Asian phenomenon (Kurlantzick, 2018).

The second reason for looking at these leaders is that they are, or were, deeply engaged in regional cooperation. All three have pursued a leading role in the creation of regional organisations or the active shaping of their policies. At first sight, this exposes the study to a potential selection bias, in the sense that we are bound to confirm the argument that populists engage in regional cooperation if we exclude those who seem to expose no particular predisposition for such cooperation. However, our thesis is not that all populist leaders necessarily engage in regional cooperation all the time. Rather, we argue that insofar as they do engage in such cooperation, their populist strategies will incentivise them to base their engagement on particular framings and preferences. If we can find common strands in these strategies across the three cases despite their differences, this will strengthen our argument that there is a common script of regional cooperation that is rooted in populism's core political logic rather than in any particular type of ideological proclivity.

The empirical analysis is based on primary analysis of official statements, speeches, interviews, and press releases by the leaders (or, in some cases, their spokespersons or subsidiary governmental bodies), as well as on previous literature. Since we are interested in populists in power, we specifically look at statements from the respective leaders' periods of incumbency – from 2010 to the present for Orbán,[3] from early 1999 to 2013 for Chávez, and from 2016 to the present for Duterte. Using online search engines and various databases such as the websites of governments and regional organisations, we purposively sampled speeches in which the leaders refer to regional or international organisations. To achieve a broad textual corpus, we included speeches delivered in different languages and directed at both international and domestic audiences.

More specifically, for Orbán we analysed speeches targeting both a domestic audience (e.g. the 'State of the Nation' addresses and speeches delivered at Hungarian universities) and international audiences such as the EU and the V4. As a supplementary source, we included Tweets by his spokesperson, as Twitter is an important part of Orbán's communication strategy. Since none of the authors speak Hungarian, we relied on the English translations of the official speeches provided by the Hungarian government. For Chávez, we analysed speeches delivered to four regional organisations[4] and to the United Nations. We relied on the original Spanish version of the speeches in this case. For Duterte, we analysed speeches delivered at summits of the Association of Southeast Asian Nations (ASEAN) and in bilateral meetings with the Chinese government, as well as speeches intended specifically for the Filipino audience, published on the website of the government of the Philippines. In the case of Duterte, the speeches were delivered in either of the two official languages of the Philippines, Tagalog and English. Because our sampling was restricted by

---

[3] To avoid distortion from contextual factors such as coalitional restraints, changes in legitimation strategies, and the international environment, we have excluded Orbán's first tenure as prime minister (1998–2002), when his Fidesz Party ruled in a coalition with the Hungarian Democratic Forum (MDF) and the Independent Smallholders' Party (FKGP).

[4] The organisations were ALBA, the Community of Latin American and Caribbean States (CELAC), the Southern Common Market (Mercosur), and the Union of South American Nations (UNASUR).

the requirements of online availability and, to some extent, English translations, we cannot claim that our analysis covers all potentially relevant sources. However, the consistency of the framing and preference patterns that emerge from the analysis along with triangulation with previous analyses strongly suggest that the included texts provide representative evidence of a populist script for regional cooperation.

In a loose adaption of frame-analysis techniques (Goffman, 1974), we carried out a close reading of the collected speeches with the objective of uncovering patterns in how the leaders represented and justified regional cooperation. In his conceptual work on populism as a discursive frame, Aslanidis (2016: 99) argues that a populist frame diagnoses reality as 'problematic because "corrupt elites" have unjustly usurped the sovereign authority of the "noble People" and maintains that the solution to the problem resides in the righteous political mobilization of the latter in order to regain power'. Guided by this general operationalisation and using the theory-based expectations about populist framings of regional cooperation as a preliminary heuristic framework, we identified relevant textual representations and justifications and synthesised them into frames. An inductive feedback loop allowed us to refine the heuristic categories where we found that the speech acts did not map onto the initial categories.

To clarify the explanatory ambitions of this framework, it should be stressed that it formulates expectations about strategies by individual leaders. Owing to the complexities of institution building, framings and institutional preferences of individual governments do not directly translate into institutional designs and policies of regional organisations. It is also clear that concrete institutional preferences will be shaped by numerous other factors, including the respective ideological outlooks of the leaders and their parties. At the same time, the potential and factual impact of populist framings and institutional preferences on regional cooperation is undeniable. In Latin America, for instance, the ALBA grouping demonstrates how populist governments can form regional alliances to facilitate their ideas about regional cooperation. Obviously, populist ideas will have a strong influence on forms of regional cooperation when a significant number of states in a region host populist governments. However, even without a numerical majority, populist governments in specific states such as Hungary may also be able to steer cooperation towards their own institutional preferences.

Predicting to what extent and under what conditions the populist script will eventually shape regionalism around the world is beyond the scope of this Element. Since our primary aim is to explore the populist script as such, rather than explaining why and when leaders employ it, we are only peripherally interested in 'non-cases'. Analysing alleged populist leaders like

British Prime Minister Boris Johnson, Indian Prime Minister Narendra Modi, or US President Donald Trump, who display no particular disposition towards regional cooperation, promises no insights into the script's distinctive patterns and political logic. That said, it is obvious that the existence of non-cooperative populists has major implications for regional cooperation and international order more broadly that demand our attention. The Conclusion (Section 9) offers some hypotheses that may explain these statesmen's lack of enthusiasm for regionalism despite the availability of the script.

4 Viktor Orbán

Viktor Orbán began his second term as Hungarian prime minister in 2010, following a landslide victory secured by his Fidesz Party, which gained a two-thirds majority in parliamentary elections. His Eurosceptic and xenophobic rhetoric, efforts to curtail pluralistic democratic institutions in Hungary, and reluctance to accept EU foreign policy orthodoxies have made him a highly polarising and controversial figure – especially within the EU political establishment in Brussels. At the same time, the Hungarian government remains deeply engaged in regional cooperation both inside and outside the EU. A manifestation of this approach is the Visegrád Group (V4), which brings together Hungary, the Czech Republic, Poland, and Slovakia. While sometimes touted as a blocking alliance against progressive policies and reforms in the EU, its member-states have often used the V4 to develop common positions and speak in solidarity on EU policies – for example, lobbying against cuts in agricultural subsidies, demanding tighter border controls, and introducing a joint approach to migration. The V4 has also assumed a pioneering role in military cooperation by establishing a Visegrád Battlegroup under the umbrella of the EU's Common Security and Defence Policy. To understand how these dynamics relate to Orbán's populist strategies, this case study analyses how the prime minister has framed Hungary's regional cooperation from 2010 onwards.

4.1 Frames

We have argued in Section 3 that the political logic of populist strategies – which constructs an antagonism between the people and the elite and portrays the leader as representing the popular will – provides the background against which populist leaders frame their representations of and judgements on regional cooperation. The three main frames are anti-liberalism, multiple and threatened identity, and popular sovereignty. The analysis shows that

Orbán's regional cooperation strategy is cast in variations of these overarching frames.

4.1.1 Illiberal Democracy

Ever since Victor Orbán became prime minister in 2010, the notion of 'illiberal democracy' has been a recurring theme in both his domestic and his foreign policy as he seeks to transform both Hungary and the EU in line with this idea (Buzogány, 2017; Enyedi, 2016; Jenne & Mudde, 2012; Krekó & Enyedi, 2018; Orbán, 2014, 2017a, 2018a; Plattner, 2019: 9–10). Orbán claims that liberal elites have distorted the meaning of European integration. He also posits that the 'liberal philosophy' is weakening Europe and forms the basis of a foreign policy system 'that is nothing less than organized hypocrisy' (Orbán, 2015). According to Orbán, the EU has rejected its *original* roots and has turned into a major actor for the advancement of the LIO, threatening *true* European principles and betraying Europe's *true* Christian values, whereas illiberalism means democracy is based on the nation-state and Christian values (Coman & Leconte, 2019: 862; Plattner, 2019: 10). While 'liberalism promotes the selfish interests of – often unpatriotic – individuals, only an illiberal democracy can devotedly serve the general interest of the whole nation' (Bíró-Nagy, 2017: 36). According to Orbán, Christian democracy is by definition anti-liberal since it is anti-immigration and prioritises Christian culture and the traditional Christian family model (Coman & Leconte, 2019: 862; Plattner, 2019: 10).

Upon its landslide election victory in 2010, Orbán's Fidesz Party used its parliamentary supermajority to push through constitutional changes that have been fiercely debated not only domestically but also within the EU body politic and in many EU member countries. It is clear that the changes violated several basic components of liberal democracy such as the principle of judicial autonomy and the freedoms of expression and religion (Plattner, 2019: 13). Addressing the European Parliament, Orbán (2012, 2013, 2017b) has claimed that constitutional changes were undertaken in Hungary to safeguard European principles and values. He firmly considers himself the vanguard of *true* European values, which have been significantly weakened by the EU's embrace of liberal principles. As evidenced by a study of Orbán's speeches, even if he is occasionally believed to be anti-EU, he is not an 'unrepentant challenger' of EU values; instead, he uses the 'plasticity of those values to style himself as a pro-European statesman, ready to steer the Union back to its moral roots' (Mos, 2020: 1).

Orbán (2015) has predicted the end of 'liberal babble', that is, detached and empty elitist discourse, claiming that he will push for a return of the national-

Christian ideology throughout Europe. In this quest, Orbán has actively tried to reform the EU and strengthen anti-liberal alliances – especially the V4 – that can be seen as a right-wing regional alliance protecting national values and identity against EU domination. The V4 has been characterised as a group with clear illiberal tendencies (Cabada, 2018: 170) that enables Poland and Hungary to mutually assist each other in 'unravelling democratic freedoms and helping normalize the illiberal environment in the region' (Higgott & Proud, 2017: 43). Importantly, however, the V4 does not constitute an alternative to the EU for Orbán, but rather a means for promoting a Central European vision in Europe (Braun, 2020; Cabada, 2018; Cabada & Waisova, 2018; Kořan, 2012). Although Orbán strongly endorses Central European cooperation through the V4, it is clear that he wants to reform the EU rather than dismantle it (see Orbán, 2016a, 2018b).

4.1.2 'Authentic Europe'

Orbán has energetically tried to foster a discourse of 'two Europes' (Coman & Leconte, 2019: 862). The first is an 'authentic' Europe, grounded on values embodied by Orbán himself and attributed to 'average' European citizens, while the second is that of an 'elitist' Europe, devoid of social depth and represented by Brussels (Coman & Leconte, 2019: 862). Hence, a *true* European identity is in permanent tension with *liberal* identity, which is accused of moving Europe into a post-Christian and postnational era by fostering pro-immigration policies, jeopardising European values and pushing towards a 'United States of Europe' (Orbán, 2017c, 2018a, 2019a). Orbán portrays himself as the bearer of the authentic European identity, 'a freedom fighter, a gatekeeper fighting for the survival of European values' (Coman & Leconte, 2019: 863). In his 2019 State of the Nation address, he warned against the dangers of a new regional world government that would abolish Hungarian and Central European identities (Orbán, 2019b), once again using Western European governments as scapegoats to convey a feeling of unity against a common threat.

Building an authentic Europe by protecting Europe's Christian roots is a core priority for Orbán, one that he believes should ultimately become a European task.[5] Orbán often quotes Robert Schumann, one of the founding fathers of the European Union, to argue that 'Europe will either be Christian or it will not exist' (Mos, 2020: 13). A steady stream of Tweets by Orbán's spokesperson, Zoltán Kovács, declares that Hungarians voted for Fidesz to stop illegal immigration, protect national sovereignty, and defend Christian culture as Europe's cultural religious foundation. In the

---

[5] Vikton Orbán's spokesperson Zoltán Kovács in a Tweet on 15 June 2019.

2016 State of the Nation address, Orbán claimed that Europe's free Christian and independent nations needed to be defended against the enemy, using the metaphor 'Europe is Hellas, not Persia; it is Rome, not Carthage; it is Christianity, not a caliphate' (Orbán, 2016b). Awarded the 'Person of the Year' award by Poland in 2016, Orbán urged the Central European nations to preserve their religious and historical national identities (Prime Minister's Office, 2016). Central Europe plays a crucial role in protecting Christian freedom against the dangers of migration (Orbán, 2019a). Clearly, migration and Christianity are intertwined, and they are both essential for strengthening Orbán's visions of an authentic Europe in both the EU and the V4.

According to Orbán, identity is not limited to nation-state boundaries but includes multiple transnational identities, with the common feature that they are jeopardised by the same threats embodied by Brussels's liberal elites that endanger the moral purity of the people. Although Orbán often frames identity and character in terms of larger civilisations, he puts considerable emphasis on the idea of 'Central Europeanness', a cohesive and fraternal Central European identity (Orbán, 2017d, 2017e). Orbán's populist rhetoric demonstrates the adoption of a new regional Central European narrative against liberal 'Western European states' (Csehi, 2019). In this sense, Orbán has transformed the notion of 'the people' from 'we, Hungarians' to 'we, (Central) Europeans', to 'we, the sovereign nations' (Csehi, 2019: 1017). The increasing cooperation within the V4 framework was contextualised within such a framing. Far more than a simple lobbying group within the EU, the V4 as presented by Orbán is a community of countries sharing a common fate, a common history, and common values (Braun, 2020: 7). After a meeting of the European Council, he claimed that no other group within the EU was as united and displayed as much solidarity as the V4 (Orbán, 2019c). Such declarations signal his intention to form a stronger East–Central European alliance that can challenge Western European mainstream parties and help him gain approval and strengthen his domestic legitimacy (Csehi, 2019: 1022).

When the European Parliament voted to pursue unprecedented disciplinary actions against Hungary in 2018, Orbán responded by claiming that Hungary had been a member of the family of Christian nations for a thousand years, that it belonged to the European family, and that its actions were intended to protect Hungary as much as Europe (Orbán, 2018c). This echoes the illiberal framing in which Orbán affirms the European project per se but rejects the way Brussels elites are 'twisting' it to corrupt authentic European values (Coman & Leconte, 2019: 856). Being tough on migrants is justified, according to Orbán, because it enables the EU to protect its way of life, whereas liberal pro-migrant policies would imperil European values and threaten European identities (Mos, 2020).

4.1.3 Europe as the Home of Nations

Another major feature of Orbán's understanding of regionalism is a strong emphasis on notions of popular sovereignty. In this sense, Orbán seeks to portray himself, along with the other V4 leaders, as willing to re-establish national popular sovereignty in the EU, taking away the power from the Brussels supranational elites and giving it back to national governments. From Orbán's perspective, Hungary is not anti-EU but rather against liberal EU politicians who disregard the nation-state and the people it represents. A key component of Orbán's narrative is that pro-migrant, federalist elites want to build an empire – the United States of Europe – that would undermine the sovereignty of Hungary and its 'honest people' (Zgut & Csehi, 2019: 1–2). It is thus key for Orbán to describe Europe as divided between sovereigntist-nationalists, like Hungary and the V4 member-states, and federalist-supranationalists, who promote regional integration at the expense of the nation-state (Orbán, 2016b, 2017c, 2018a, 2018d). In his 2019 State of the Nation address, Orbán played on fears of sovereignty being compromised and implicitly accused the EU of trying to dismantle the nation-state (Orbán, 2019b).

Orbán fiercely advocates for a return of national competences to the member countries, stressing the need for Europe to be an alliance of free nations based on sovereignty (Jozwiak, 2017: 2; Orbán, 2018b). Hence, sovereignty does not equate to a lack of cooperation. This is evidenced by various slogans such as 'We need the EU and the EU needs us' (About Hungary, 2018); 'We are Europe' (*Miniszterelnok.hu,* 2019); 'While we serve the nation, our place is in Europe' (Hungary Today, 2018); and 'Europe is the home of nations' (Hungary Journal, 2018). Similarly, the 2019 initiative to strengthen cooperation between Hungary (together with the other V4 states) and Estonia was placed under the motto of 'Sovereignty Within the European Union' (Daily News Hungary, 2019). These catchphrases reveal a vision of regional cooperation as enhancing rather than constraining expressions of national self-determination.

However, this vision is under continual threat by corrupt institutions and politicians who fail to respect popular demands. Despite his government's xenophobic ideology, Orbán (2017f) claims that the 'main threat to the future of Europe are not those who want to come here to live, but our own political, economic and intellectual elites bent on transforming Europe against the will of the European people'. In Orbán's speech acts, the V4 represents both the Central European peoples who were deprived of their sovereignty *and* the vanguard in the effort to (re-)establish sovereignty in European politics, because, unlike Western European countries, the V4 countries value their independence above anything else (Orbán, 2019d). He insisted that the V4 countries would only support individuals who respect Europe's nations as candidates for membership of the EU Commission or the position of Council president (Kovács, 2019; Orbán, 2018d). In his 2020 State of the Nation address, he claimed that history had given the peoples of Central Europe the opportunity to build a new system of alliances based on their own national interests, and that, by protecting the sovereign rights of the people, Hungary embodied the future of Europe (Orbán, 2020). Thus, regional cooperation clearly functions as an extension of the domestic populist strategy of legitimating the leader as the representative of the people's will.

4.2 Institutional Preferences

The framings identified privilege certain interpretations of what is at stake in regional cooperation, advance specific problem definitions, and highlight potential solutions while excluding alternative points of view. They thus shape the institutional preferences of the Orbán government. Moreover, Orbán's framings of regional cooperation fit into his populist strategies by representing the collaboration of the V4 countries as a fight among peoples sharing common values to regain their lost autonomy from a foreign elite. From within this set of frames, certain institutional forms appear as preferable to those prescribed by the conventional, liberal script of regional integration, which relies on the delegation and pooling of authority, supranational governance for the provision of public goods, and functional spill overs from one policy field to another.

4.2.1 Leader-Driven Intergovernmentalism

The Orbán government favours intergovernmental regional institutions driven by the executives of the member-states over supranational ones. Accordingly, Orbán criticises progressive regional integration in the EU while strenuously supporting the Central European V4 model of cooperation between strong sovereign states. While lower-level and more technical cooperation between ministerial bureaucracies or within commissions is not completely rejected, interaction at the level of heads of government takes on a crucial role in Orbán's vision.

Cabada (2018: 167) argues that Central European states use their various non-formal cooperation formats, such as the V4, primarily to promote their own national interests. In particular, the leaders favour an intergovernmental design that creates ample space to manoeuvre for personalistic leadership. This is evidenced by the fact that Orbán presents himself as the informal leader of Central Europe within the EU (Jozwiak, 2016). As elaborated earlier, Orbán repeatedly speaks out against supranationalism and urges the EU to give back control to member-state governments. As Hungarian Minister of Foreign Affairs Péter Szijjártó indicates, 'there are those who believe that a strong European Union can only be built on weak member-states, and if the competences of member-states are collected in a central body, but in Hungary's view a strong EU can only be built on strong member-states' (Szijjártó, 2018). By contrast, the V4 is strictly intergovernmental, works on consensus, and relies on interpersonal links between leaders. The dominance of intergovernmental cooperation and the absence of common positions shared by the four countries on many important issues allow national leaders to retain maximum control. This preference for flexibility echoes Orbán's criticism of supranational institutions that ostensibly dilute the representation of the popular will. It also allows him to enact his role as the guardian of popular sovereignty and the legitimate decision-maker on behalf of, and for the benefit of, the nation.

4.2.2 Symbols, Branding, and Mutual Legitimation

To Orbán's government, regional cooperation seems to provide a stage in which like-minded governments can express mutual solidarity and legitimise each other in the eyes of both the international and the domestic communities. Against this primary goal, problem-solving policymaking becomes a secondary goal of cooperation. The V4 is the main instrument for Orbán in this regard. It provides him with a 'regional brand' that not only amplifies his positions in Brussels policymaking circles but also supports his domestic political strategies by allowing him to enact the role of a strongman and 'man of the people'.

The activities and narratives of the V4 serve both as a mutual legitimation tool and as a way of building a sense of common identity (Braun, 2020). Through joint speeches, award ceremonies, and public declarations of solidarity and unity, its leaders create a brand promoting national and Central European interests in the EU and the rest of the world. In particular, they politicise cooperation to fend off external criticism, while substantial policymaking goals recede into the background (Jozwiak, 2016). A prime example is Orbán's support for the Polish government when it came under pressure from

Brussels for allegedly undermining liberal democratic institutions. Orbán (2019d) retorted that any attack against a Central European state amounts to an attack against Central Europe as a whole. In its turn, the Polish government awarded its 2016 Person of the Year award to the Hungarian prime minister (Prime Minister's Office, 2016). Such reciprocal displays of solidarity aim at strengthening an anti-liberal alliance in Europe and harnessing mutual support. Arguably, more than pursuing concrete goals, Orbán seeks to instrumentalise the V4 to create an image of unprecedented unity among the four Central European countries in the bloc (Jozwiak, 2017). This common outlook, Orbán says, has turned the V4 countries into the most secure and economically flourishing region in Europe (see Orbán, 2016a, 2019e). Such claims to success are supposed to legitimate his authority at home and internationally. These and similar expressions have a high symbolic value and stress the solidarity and common roots that form the basis of the regional alliance. At the same time, Orbán also uses his government's role in the V4 to project Hungary's position as a regional leader to his domestic audience (Jozwiak, 2017).

Apart from its purpose as a stage for mutual legitimation, 'Visegrad offers its four members a useful model to discuss and represent common interests in a collective manner within the regional and international political landscape' (Törő et al., 2014: 365). In this regard, the V4 acts as an amplifier for its member-states' interests in Brussels and around the world (Kořan, 2012; Nič, 2016; Tulmets, 2014). The purpose of showing a common front obscures the fact that the V4 is a fairly loose partnership or 'concert of sovereign states' (Törő et al., 2014: 391; see also Kořan, 2012), in which governments cooperate only when appropriate without being bound to exclusive policy positions. For example, the Hungarian government has stressed the unity of the V4 on issues such as migration even though the interests of the V4 countries clash on many important matters (Kořan, 2012: 206). This confirms the primarily symbolic nature of the alliance.

4.2.3 Selective Cooperation

While emphasising the symbolic value of regional cooperation, Orbán's approach to regional cooperation seeks tangible gains on a selected number of issues. Accordingly, the V4 does not have an issue-specific cooperation format. While it nominally covers a broad range of issues, substantial cooperation ultimately only develops on select issues of common interest to its member-states (Cabada & Waisova, 2018: 13). Orbán and his fellow populist leaders opportunistically pursue cooperation on issues that fit their domestic strategies. Orbán has pushed the fight against illegal immigration and more restrictive asylum policies to the top of the V4 agenda (Orbán, 2019e, 2019 f). Indeed, many analysts regard formulating a common standpoint on illegal immigration to increase their negotiating weight in the EU as one of the main drivers of closer cooperation among the bloc's members (Bauerová, 2018: 101; Braun, 2020; Cabada & Waisova, 2018; Puzyniak, 2018). It was only during the so-called refugee crisis in 2015 that it became a primary internal legitimation discourse in Hungary (and, to some extent, Poland), thus sharpening the V4's profile in European politics (Cabada & Waisova, 2018: 11; Hokovsky, 2017: 53). Using the V4 as a lobbying group in EU institutions, both Budapest and Warsaw expressed their opposition to a relocation scheme for refugees (Puzyniak, 2018: 237). Preventing migration is also one of the aims behind the Hungarian government's support for enhanced EU cooperation in the defence sector (Gotkowska, 2017).

Migration has also become a constant feature in the majority of Orbán's speeches at EU summits. While the Hungarian strategy in the EU cannot be reduced to fighting immigration, the topic has come to dominate Hungary's perspective on European politics (Inotai, 2019). The government's exceptional focus is justified by constructing immigration as a threat to Hungarian identity and sovereignty. Orbán has repeatedly called immigration the most important European issue and has expressed his hope of finding EU partners who share the Hungarian position (Orbán, 2019g). In this context, he welcomed the election of Ursula von der Leyen as president of the European Commission, in the expect-ation that she would promote more reasonable debate about immigration within the EU (Orbán, 2019h) . Orbán also expressed support for and satisfaction over the nomination of Hungarian diplomat László Trócsányi as EU Commissioner for the Neighbourhood Policy in Von der Leyen's cabinet since his portfolio covered relations with important transit states. For the Hungarian government, the nomination was a chance to upgrade the interests of Central Europeans in protecting the 'European Way of Life' and 'Christian Culture' (Orbán, 2019c, 2019 g, 2019i, 2019j). When the European Parliament's Legal Affairs Committee, which cited concerns about a conflict of interest, dismissed Trócsányi's candidacy, Orbán accused the Parliament of having political motives (Gurzu et al., 2019).

5 Hugo Chávez

Hugo Chávez is perhaps the most well-known proponent of the 'Pink Tide' left-wing populism that swept Latin America in the early 2000s. As Venezuelan president from 1999 until his death in 2013, he developed a foreign policy that was aimed at reducing US hegemony and had a pronounced regional component. In particular, Chávez devised the Bolivarian Alliance for the Peoples of Our America (ALBA), which brought together left-leaning governments from twelve states of Central and South America as well as the Caribbean.[6] In the centre of Chávez's regional integration strategy was the implementation of ALBA. For this reason, the alliance forms the core of the present analysis. However, his relation to other regional organisations will also be included at different points to enable a more complete picture.

5.1 Frames

Chávez's regional cooperation strategy is a vivid example of how leaders can externalise the populist logic beyond national boundaries to maintain political support upon being elected. His left-wing brand of populism has a distinctive internationalist dimension. This translates into his framing of regional cooperation, which shows strong traces of anti-liberalism, multiple identity constructions, and notions of popular sovereignty.

5.1.1 Anti-Imperialism

Anti-imperialism and anti-hegemonism, in combination with a particular kind of pan-Americanism, were core features of Chávez's foreign policy (Dodson & Dorraj, 2008: 76; Hawkins, 2016). They could be derived from 'Chavismo', the broader ideological framework that mixed left-wing policies with patriotism and authoritarian tendencies on which the leader built his political career (Wajner & Roninger, 2019). Chávez attacked the US on the grounds that its neoliberal-imposed policies – represented by the Free Trade Area of the Americas (FTAA) and the Organization of American States (OAS) – were elitist and predatory (Dodson & Dorraj, 2008; Wajner & Roniger, 2019: 6) and part of US hegemonic power. However, Chávez's regional strategy did not just aim to undermine US hemispheric institutionalism; it also fostered the creation of a new regional institutional architecture with the clear objective of excluding the United States (Romero & Mijares, 2016: 183). To this end, Chávez actively pursued the creation of ALBA and the Community of Latin American and Caribbean States (CELAC), withdrew from the Andean Community (CAN), participated in the creation of the Union of South American Nations (UNASUR), and joined Mercosur (the Southern Common Market) to advance a geopolitical shift of regional states away from the United States (Serbin & Pont, 2017: 234). Furthermore, he played a fundamental role in

---

[6] The list of present and former members includes Antigua and Barbuda, Bolivia, Cuba, Dominica, Ecuador, Grenada, Honduras, Nicaragua, Saint Kitts and Nevis, Saint Lucia, St Vincent and the Grenadines, and Venezuela.

the collapse of the FTAA negotiations (Brown, 2010: 86) – which he considered an abuse of sovereignty and a colonial imperialist plan (Guevara, 2005: 101–102) – as well as in the demolition of the hemispheric governance capability of the OAS (Romero & Mijares, 2016: 183).

Chávez's anti-liberalism stance becomes evident in many official speeches, where a heavy anti-US rhetoric was used to dismiss critiques coming from North America and to legitimise left-wing Latin American regimes, both domestically and internationally (Burges, 2007; Sylvia & Danopoulos, 2003). For example, in a famous speech delivered to the United Nations (UN) General Assembly in 2006, Chávez referred to US imperialism as the 'greatest threat looming over our planet' and labelled President George W. Bush as 'the devil' (Brown, 2010: 86).

Chávez stated that Latin American unity was the only way to defeat imperialism (Chávez, 2005). He initiated ALBA as a counter-project to US influence in Latin America. In their speech at the inauguration of ALBA, both Chávez and Cuban leader Fidel Castro recalled the colonial history of Latin America and established ALBA as a new kind of regional integration that would strengthen Latin American sovereignty and independence by setting the region free from any undue external interference – that is, the United States (Chávez & Castro, 2004). Furthermore, contrary to the liberal notion of comparative advantage embodied in the FTAA, ALBA was based on the concept of 'cooperative advantage'. This notion identified equal trade relations and fair distribution of benefits among all social groups – instead of profit maximisation for the economic elites – as the main purpose of economic exchange (Christensen, 2007: 142; Gürcan, 2019: 98). Chávez was also active in the creation of UNASUR. Similar to ALBA, UNASUR represented an attempt to create an alternative to the liberal model (Bilotta, 2018), while it also tried to exclude the United States from playing a role in the resolution of regional conflicts and to create a regional model outside of US hegemony (Garcia, 2012: 74–5).

In April 2006, Chávez decided to withdraw from the CAN, accusing Colombia and Peru of 'killing the bloc' (Němec, 2007: 84) by signing free trade treaties with the United States. In fact, he believed that the CAN would soon become a small FTAA (Malamud, 2006: 2–3). Merely three months later, Chávez expressed his intention to join Mercosur, with the strategic objective of moving the bloc away from neoliberalism and making it more like ALBA (Carranza, 2010: 9–11; see also Brown, 2010; Gardini, 2011; Gouvea & Montoya, 2014; Ruiz, 2006). Even if Mercosur in its early years was 'a creature of the Washington Consensus' (Garcia, 2012: 71), promoting primarily a neoliberal agenda (Garcia, 2012; Gardini, 2011), Chávez aimed to transform it into a political project with the goal of challenging US hegemony and unifying Latin America beyond the liberal model (Brown, 2010; Carranza, 2010). In 2012, when Venezuela officially joined Mercosur, Chávez hailed this success as a 'defeat to American imperialism' (Bastenier, 2012) and proudly stated that he was going to 'politicise Mercosur', steering it towards anti-liberalism (AP Archive, 2015; Ruiz, 2006). The same rationale underlay his involvement in the creation of CELAC in 2011, which he positioned as a Latin American organisation, free of any US influence, that would replace the OAS (Europa Press, 2011).

5.1.2 Nuestramérica

Wajner and Roniger (2019: 10) argue that 'Chavismo's frameworks of regionalism were the first to propose both rhetorically and practically a transnational identity.' Chávez stressed a common Latin American identity that transcends state boundaries by drawing on Simón Bolívar's dream of a Pan-American identity and engaging in regional initiatives to pursue closer integration among Latin American countries (Dodson & Dorraj, 2008). The roots for such a common sense of belonging were embedded in the notion of 'Americanismo', the idea that the common (and ongoing) anti-colonial struggle of many Latin American countries would unite different ethnic groups and multiple identities (Mudde & Rovira Kaltwasser, 2011). Reviving this narrative of solidarity against a common enemy, Chávez legitimated regional cooperation by referring to Latin America as 'Our America' (*Nuestramérica*) in opposition to the 'imperialist and expansionist' North America, thus countering the *divide et impera* efforts of the United States (Wajner & Roniger, 2019). Although ALBA best represents the construction of a regional organisation whose appeal is based on shared values, history, and culture, the threat by an external force (namely, the United States) was a core feature of Chávez's interactions with other countries in the region. Hence, the strong focus on solidarity aimed to reduce asymmetries and to help create internal cohesion among countries that shared similar histories and values (Christensen, 2007). More than a regional project, ALBA was an ideology, a concept inspired by the Bolivarian ideals of Latin American political unity, solidarity, and endogenous development (Alaniz, 2013; Gardini, 2011).

The existence of multiple and threatened identities is demonstrated in many official speeches Chávez delivered in domestic, regional, and international settings. From the very first ALBA Summit in 2004, the presidents of Cuba and Venezuela stressed the concept of 'solidarity' among the organisation's members, invoking the ideas of Bolívar and all those who had the dream of creating a shared Latin American homeland – ALBA was repeatedly referred to as 'our homeland' (Chávez & Castro, 2004; Telesur, 2012). Such notions of identity transcended traditional and strictly geographical connotations. During the 3rd ALBA Summit, Chávez included Mexico, even though it was not a member of ALBA and geographically part of North America. This flexible attitude to participation demonstrates the intent to build a multilayered and inclusive identity encompassing a community that goes beyond national borders.

The creation of UNASUR was strongly based on the commitment to 'consolidate a South American identity' (Garcia, 2012: 80). The emphasis on identity politics was central in the discourse and practices of UNASUR, particularly when the *pro tempore* presidency fell to governments supportive of Chavismo (Wajner & Roniger, 2019). Furthermore, when Venezuela joined Mercosur, one of the objectives of the Venezuelan president was to create a South American identity and a bloc based on solidarity and cooperation (Carranza, 2010; Ruiz, 2006). In fact, Mercosur 'became the ideological site that could preserve a common vision of Latinidad while also attending to the complicated and contradictory ways these identity politics interacted with global forces' (Gouvea & Montoya, 2014: 565). According to Ruiz (2006: 105), Chávez intended to use ALBA as a model to inspire the 'new Mercosur', particularly for matters that concerned Latin American identity and solidarity. During his speech on the occasion of Venezuela's admission to Mercosur, Chávez recalled the shared history of *Nuestramérica* through references to Latin American heroes (Simón Bolívar, José Martí) and referred to Latin America as the 'Great Homeland', 'Queen of Nations', 'Great Republic', and 'Great Nation' (NTN24, 2012). In 2012, former Venezuelan Chancellor Nicolás Maduro argued that 'Nuestramérica finds the path of Our Libertadores consolidating systems such as ALBA, UNASUR and CELAC ... looking for a path in diversity [that respects diversity, while defining] common economic, cultural and political projects' (Wajner & Roniger, 2019: 16). Similar declarations were made during the 2013 CELAC Summit, in which Chávez recalled the past of common struggles and pride that united Latin American countries (Chávez, 2013). Clearly, this rhetoric signals the coexistence of a multiplicity of identities that Chávez managed to reconcile and bring together in an effort to build a strong, united, Latin American regional bloc.

5.1.3 Regionalism for the People

Although Chávez placed great emphasis on a shared homeland, appeals to popular sovereignty represented the real strength of Chávez's regional cooperation. By addressing a region that had been heavily marked by a colonial past, Chávez wanted to promote himself as the one who would bring sovereignty back to the Latin American people.

Among the several regional projects in which Venezuela took a leadership role, ALBA was built with the clear intention of safeguarding and enhancing the leader's proclaimed role in taking back control from the elites represented by the neoliberal corporate model promoted by the United States. During its first summit, Chávez and Castro made it clear that ALBA would foster integration while preserving national sovereignty and independence. During the 7th ALBA Summit, Chávez and the other regional leaders established a Permanent Committee on Sovereignty and Defence. Moreover, respect for national sovereignty is affirmed throughout the formal agreements signed within the ALBA framework (i.e. Article 2 of the People's Trade Agreement (TCP)). This emphasis on sovereignty does not contradict the promotion of a shared regional identity, as it encapsulates the idea of a joint response to a hegemonic model of regionalism that is perceived as weakening national sovereignty and autonomy (Cusack, 2019: 97). It is also not an entirely statist notion. In essence, ALBA sought to reinforce the self-determination and sovereignty of Latin American peoples by presenting a plan of integration that would counteract hegemonic economic policies of the United States, the World Bank, and the International Monetary Fund (IMF).

Chávez's appeal to popular sovereignty also informed his strategies of engagement with and withdrawal from various regional organisations. When Venezuela terminated its membership in the CAN, Chávez claimed that 'it made no sense for Venezuela to remain in the CAN, a body which serves only the elites and transnational companies and not "our people"' (Malamud, 2006: 2). Likewise, he justified the decision to join Mercosur by arguing for regionalism in the interest of 'the people' while leaving 'the old elitist corporate model of integration' behind (Carranza, 2010: 8).

5.2 Institutional Preferences

Through the presented frames, the former Venezuelan president integrated his regional cooperation policies into his political project of Chavismo. The populist logic of this vision is clearly identifiable in the juxtaposition of US hegemony (the elite) with the collective identity of *Nuestramérica* (the people) and the promise of a regionalist structure for the benefit of the 'common folk' (the 'will of the people'). These frames crucially shaped his government's strategies regarding the institutionalisation of regional cooperation.

5.2.1 Presidentialism

A first notable feature of Chávez's institutional preferences was the paramount importance of intergovernmental formats in which he could exert maximum influence and project his image as a regional leader (Jácome, 2012: 83). The general 'presidentialist' orientation of his foreign policy (Serbin & Pont, 2017) thus extended to his approach to regional cooperation. Thanks to their largely intergovernmental design, ALBA, UNASUR, CELAC, and to a lesser extent Mercosur offered Chávez the opportunity to significantly steer their agendas according to his personal preferences.

Since Chávez himself created ALBA, he clearly was the key actor and spokesperson of the organisation. ALBA's institutional design directly served the political will of the presidents (Altmann-Borbón, 2019; Ruiz, 2012). This diffuse and loose type of regional organisation was deliberately constructed in a way that maximised Chávez's influence. Cusack (2019: 50) calls it a case of 'dissimulative regionalism', whereby lip service to formal structures and procedures veils the fact that they are effectively insignificant and decisions are taken informally according to the whims of the president. ALBA thus operates more as a 'brand governance' that seeks to present regional preferences as part of a coherent and unitary scheme (Cusack, 2019: 17–28).

The importance of ALBA as Chávez's brainchild should not obscure the fact that he had a fundamentally pragmatic stance towards regional cooperation, and that he engaged in forum shopping across Latin America's multiple overlapping regional organisations to maximise his influence. Accordingly, some authors have interpreted Chávez's strategies of engagement and disengagement as 'strategic regionalism' (Quiliconi & Salgado Espinoza, 2017; Ruiz, 2006). For example, in 2006, his government announced the disengagement from two cooperation schemes – the CAN and the *Grupo de los Tres* (G-3) – owing to political divergences with the main cooperation partners in these forums. Instead, Venezuela's bid to become a member of Mercosur reflected changing perceptions of the relative benefits of participating in different initiatives. Mercosur lacks a significant supranational agency and is characterised by intergovernmental cooperation that extends substantial latitude to heads of state (Mothiane, 2016; Ruiz-Dana et al., 2007). Realising that not all Latin American states would join ALBA under his leadership, Chávez tried to turn Mercosur against the United States (Gardini, 2011; Serbin & Pont, 2017). However, whereas members of ALBA, UNASUR, and CELAC broadly shared Chávez's anti-imperialist framing, the broad membership composition of Mercosur made it difficult for Chávez to advance his own interests in the organisation's presidential diplomacy (Němec, 2007: 85). Chávez was therefore initially eager to support Brazil's proposal for a new regional framework that eventually led to the formation of UNASUR in 2008. However, when Chávez failed to project his leadership in this new initiative, he set out to establish yet another regional organisation:

CELAC (Wajner & Roniger, 2019: 7–8). Much like ALBA, CELAC was mostly a political project that allowed Latin American presidents to shape the agenda according to their political strategic goals (Gouvea & Montoya, 2014; Quiliconi & Salgado Espinoza, 2017). The bloc also reflected the preference for intergovernmentalist designs. As a non-institutionalised consultation mechanism, it did not require member-states to cede any of their sovereignty (Quiliconi & Salgado Espinoza, 2017: 21–2).

5.2.2 Symbols, Propaganda, and 'Revolution'

For Chávez, regional cooperation provided a stage for performative acts that enhanced regime legitimacy. Highly symbolic performances of a particular, dramatic style – militaristic rhetoric, metaphorical language, and references to anti-colonial heroes – reproduced the antagonism between the Latin American people and the imperialist, neoliberal elites. Regional cooperation thus acquired a value independent from its concrete problem-solving capacities.

Chávez's populist strategy was based on a strong symbolism that was linked to his charismatic personality and a unique rhetoric. His speeches and declarations were infused with militaristic tropes ('bury imperialist form of regionalism', 'homeland or death'), as well as metaphors or quotes invoking a shared Latin American heritage represented by personalities such as Simón Bolívar or Che Guevara (Chávez, 2005; Wajner & Roniger, 2019: 4). By associating the regional project with anti-imperialist heroes and liberation wars, Chávez was able to pursue the aim of regional community building while also bolstering support for his leadership at home.

For Chávez, as well as for other heads of state, ALBA represented a regional facilitator of vital mutual support for besieged leaders (Cusack, 2019). Quiliconi and Salgado Espinoza (2017: 32) suggest that 'this initiative has never constituted a traditional economic integration … but it was nonetheless a platform through which Chávez projected his power in the region based on shared ideological identities'. The ALBA Summits were clearly geared towards legitimating member-states' governments by appealing to the common past struggles to set the region free from hegemonic powers and by dismissing any criticism as hegemonically or colonially connotated. Primary examples are displays of support by Chávez and fellow ALBA leaders for Bolivian President Evo Morales, who faced domestic unrest and protests between 2006 and 2008; Honduran President Manuel Zelaya, who was ousted in a coup after attempting to circumvent constitutional restraints to foster his rule in 2009; and the regime in Cuba, which Chávez thought had an unjustified embargo levied against it (ALBA 2008, 2009; Gardner, 2009). In turn, the Venezuelan president relied on support from his fellow heads of state after increased criticism in the aftermath of the 2007 elections (Jácome, 2012). It is no wonder, then, that critical observers view ALBA as a political forum and propaganda tool (Němec, 2007: 85).

The same symbolic performances characterise Chávez's participation in other regional initiatives. UNASUR helped build an important political space through which South American countries could successfully sideline the United States in the articulation and management of the regional political agenda (Chodor & McCarthy-Jones, 2013: 217). Chávez called UNASUR Latin America's 'armour against barbarism' and 'the most reliable guarantee that providence can give us so that we can assure the continuity of our republics and South American independence' (Chodor & McCarthy-Jones, 2013: 217; El 19, 2015). When it was clear that ALBA had become a stagnant organisation, Chávez viewed CELAC as an initiative in which his regional vision could gain greater internal and external legitimacy (Wajner & Roniger, 2019). At the 2nd CELAC Summit in 2013, Chávez invoked the glorious past of the anti-imperialist liberators to offer a strong basis for the legitimation of his foreign policy (Chávez, 2013). Even though Mercosur was more of an economic project, Chávez tried to infuse it with the same strong symbolic and discursive elements that characterised his populist rhetoric. Similar to ALBA, Mercosur was malleable to every variety of compromise without real content, which facilitated Chávez's forum-shopping strategies when it became clear that it was the most enduring project in Latin America (Gardini, 2011: 698). According to some scholars, the influence of Chavismo transformed Mercosur from a chiefly commercial bloc into a more ideological one (Franco, 2012).

5.2.3 Tactics and Cherry-Picking

Chávez pursued a highly selective and flexible cooperation approach both within and beyond ALBA. While prioritising the symbolic aspect of regionalism, he also pushed for output-oriented collaboration on certain policy fields. In a sense, the very creation of ALBA reflected this selective approach. Promising cooperation, ALBA offered a broad range of issues; however, as several authors note, it was ultimately designed to enable specific transactions in support of its member governments' domestic legitimation strategies. For example, Chávez drew on Venezuela's vast oil resources to finance a variety of regional cooperation projects benefiting the poor – a central constituency for ALBA's left-wing governments – in education, the health sector, and agriculture (Wajner & Roniger, 2019: 10). Some observers argue that facilitating the exchange of

Venezuelan oil for Cuban doctors was one, if not *the,* main purpose of ALBA (Chodor & McCarthy-Jones, 2013: 220; Looney, 2018).

Chávez also used his financial leverage to cherry-pick initiatives that would directly serve what he saw as the geostrategic purpose of ALBA, namely, countering the hegemonic power of the United States. This explains ALBA's emphasis on energy projects that would ensure regional 'energy sovereignty' (Wajner & Roniger, 2019: 8–11). Chávez's critical stance towards the United States also provided a rationale for initiatives aimed at increasing financial independence from neoliberal global governance institutions, including plans for a regional currency and the establishment of the ALBA Bank, which was created to promote social and economic development independently of the IMF and the World Bank (De la Fuente, 2011). Anti-US sentiments were also drivers behind Venezuela's financial support for Telesur as a regional media outlet.

Substantial cooperation in different policy fields often followed *ad hoc* tactical considerations rather than a broader strategy of institutionalisation according to functional demands. For example, when the United States stopped buying soybeans from Bolivia in 2006, Cuba and Venezuela began importing them under ALBA. In 2007, when Daniel Ortega entered his second term as president of Nicaragua, he received several million US dollars worth of aid from Venezuela. Similar policies aimed at reducing dependence on the United States were launched for Ecuador and even for non-member-states, such as Paraguay, St Kitts and Nevis, Haiti, and the Dominican Republic. These initiatives first and foremost served the purpose of creating allies who could potentially join the anti-US regional bloc. The ALBA Bank was created as a non-capitalist political instrument for social and economic development and an alternative mechanism to the IMF, the World Bank, and the perceived influence of the United States (De la Fuente, 2011).

6 Rodrigo Duterte

Rodrigo Duterte was elected president of the Philippines in 2016. Although politicians in other Southeast Asian countries (such as Indonesia and Thailand) have also successfully adopted populist strategies in recent years (Kenny, 2018), Duterte is arguably the leader most commonly associated with the rise of populism in the region. His regional foreign policy provides us with evidence that the patterns of populist approaches to regional cooperation apply beyond Europe and Latin America – the two regions that have been the main focus of research on populism as a regional phenomenon. The following analysis unpacks Duterte's framings and institutional preferences in terms of regional cooperation in the context of both his engagement with ASEAN and his relations with China.

6.1 Frames

It has been argued that populism in Southeast Asia has features that are fundamentally different from those of populism in Europe and the Americas (Kenny, 2018; Kurlantzick, 2018). We are not denying that Duterte forges his particular brand of populism using distinctive narratives. At the same time, we also observe that the logic of populism as a generic political strategy leads him to frame regional cooperation in ways that are in some respects quite similar to those of Orbán and Chávez.

6.1.1 Anti-Cosmopolitanism

Duterte's foreign policy frames are built on a strong component of anti-liberalism in at least two main ways (Arugay, 2018). On the one hand, he explicitly criticises established liberal powers, the United States in particular, and institutions of the LIO, especially the UN (Heydarian, 2018; Teehankee, 2016). On the other hand, his anti-liberal stance is reinforced though intensified collaboration with anti-liberal powers, especially China and, to a lesser extent, Russia.

From his first day in office, Duterte made clear that he would put Philippine foreign policy on a new course, away from the traditional US dependency (Heydarian, 2018: 43). The Philippine leader did not only challenge the country's oldest allies but also questioned its long-standing commitment to the LIO (Heydarian, 2018; Magcamit, 2018). Duterte's political strategy is illiberal in the sense that he views human rights as particular rather than universal and staunchly opposes their imposition upon Asian nations (Curato, 2017: 16). This framing resonates with the historical roots of ASEAN, a regional project that is to a considerable extent directed towards strengthening regional regimes against external interference, which includes attempts at instilling a democratisation agenda into the organisation (Juego, 2017). Drawing on these traditions, Duterte has frequently called for stronger ASEAN cooperation, in particular in fighting the illegal drugs trade. He thus positions regional cooperation as a counterweight to Western meddling, as the Obama administration and the EU vociferously accused the Philippine government of violating human rights in its 'war on drugs' (ABS-CBN News, 2017; Duterte, 2017a, 2019a; Paterno, 2016; Ranada, 2017). Duterte has repeatedly rebuked such charges and has criticised the double standards and patronising attitude of the West (Duterte, 2016b; Gita, 2016; Lacorte, 2016;

Ross, 2017; Roughneen & Smith, 2018). Tellingly, relations with the United States have somewhat improved after the right-wing populist Donald Trump, whose opinion on his Philippine counterpart was considerably more benign, replaced the liberal Barack Obama as president. How bilateral ties develop after Trump's departure will largely depend on whether the Biden administration chooses to take a pragmatic approach of maintaining strategic alliances or play up its liberal profile as a human rights champion in the Indo-Pacific region (Calayag, 2021).

While openly challenging liberal Western values, Duterte also initiated a foreign policy shift towards China and Russia (Heydarian, 2018). During the ASEAN Summit, when he officially took over the regional body's chairpersonship, Duterte declared a radical reorientation of Philippine foreign policy: 'I am ready to not really break ties [with the United States] but we will open alliances with China and... Medvedev [i.e. Russia]' (Heydarian, 2018: 47). Heydarian (2018: 52) refers to Duterte as an 'American skeptic and China dove'. The rapprochement with China is partially founded on a shared disdain for Western concerns with human rights (East Asia Forum, 2017). In a clear break from the former ally, Duterte claimed to 'talk more candidly with the Chinese than with Americans' (Baviera, 2016: 203). This separation from the liberal world aims to create a new strategic balance in the region (De Castro, 2019). As a matter of fact, Duterte's positive stance towards China could convince other countries to engage with the regime and signal new and more robust ASEAN–China relations to contrast US influence in the region (Chongkittavorn, 2016). Indeed, Duterte tried to reconcile ASEAN with China, especially concerning the territorial conflicts in the South China Sea, where Duterte departed from the antagonist foreign policy of his predecessor and adopted a more conciliatory tone (Duterte, 2018). At a 2016 summit in Laos, Duterte followed the Chinese line that the issue was a purely bilateral one, thereby dissociating himself from the United States, which had attempted to leverage regional opposition to Chinese claims (De Castro, 2019). Generally speaking, Duterte's foreign policy is not aimed at disengaging from regional partnerships, rather at redirecting them to fit his anti-liberal strategies (Heydarian, 2018: 98).

6.1.2 Philippine Nationalism and the ASEAN 'Family'

Although less obviously than Orbán and Chávez, Duterte also plays up regional identity politics. His speech acts appeal to a multiplicity of identities (Philippine, ASEAN, and Chinese) that face a common threat from the imperial West, represented primarily by the United States and the institutions of the LIO. Duterte's populism is certainly built on a strong sense of Filipino nationalism, which has increasingly taken on an anti-American flavour that not only stems from the more recent confrontations over the war on drugs but is also deeply rooted in historical grievances and anti-colonial sentiments (Ileto, 1993: 78; Teehankee, 2016). However, Filipino nationalism does not preclude broader regional identities. In fact, Duterte has invoked the notion of 'Asian values' (Heydarian, 2018), a concept advanced by Asian intellectuals and politicians in the 1990s to emphasise distinctive regional civilisational traits and to challenge the universal validity and superiority of the liberal-democratic ideas that buttressed the LIO. The confident promotion and fusion of national and regional identities is somewhat surprising if we consider that, historically, 'Filipino nationalism was isolated from the more radical Pan-Asian nationalism and was treated as a pariah due to its dominating neo-colonial relationship with the US' (Teehankee, 2016: 84).

When the Philippines assumed the chair of ASEAN in 2017, Duterte claimed that the main goal during his term as chair would be 'consolidating our community for our peoples, with a sense of togetherness and common identity; ready and able to take our rightful place in the global community of nations' (Duterte, 2017b: 1). At the opening ceremony, he used the expressions 'our ASEAN brothers' and 'ASEAN family' to reiterate the belonging to a common shared identity. These performances served 'to promote the work of the country's controversial president and underline the leading role of the country in articulating and performing political and imagined pan-ASEAN identities' (Peterson & Maiquez, 2020: 36). These formulations resonate with ASEAN's proclaimed community slogan of 'Unity in Diversity'. On many occasions and in many speeches, Duterte emphasises ASEAN centrality, unity, and solidarity, as well as a sense of togetherness and common identity (Duterte, 2016a; 2017a; ERIA, 2017).

Chinese identity adds a third layer to Duterte's identity politics, which he has used to support closer relations with Beijing. In an interview with the Chinese state broadcaster China Central Television, Duterte claimed 'I am Chinese', adding that one quarter of the Philippine population was of Chinese descent (Huang & Steger, 2016). This suggests that domestic imperatives surrounding nationalism and identity formed the background to Duterte's swift change of Philippine foreign policy. It comes as no surprise that Duterte's identitarian claims towards China are linked to his opposition to the United States.

6.1.3 People-Oriented Community

Duterte represents regional cooperation in the ASEAN framework and the ties between the Philippines and China as a means of preserving the independence of the Philippines against the United States as the former colonial power, and of regaining the autonomy of its people. It is a declared priority of the Philippine government to promote ASEAN as a mode of regionalism and a global player in the international arena. Arguably, these goals correspond to Duterte's claims to enhance both the internal and the external sovereignty of the Philippines through regional cooperation. Indeed, ever since the beginning of his mandate, Duterte has promised to reorient the country's foreign relations towards national interests and the benefit of ordinary citizens (Arugay, 2018). At the 13th ASEAN Business Summit, Duterte pointed to the need to reconcile the bloc's community-building project with the national interests of its member-states. At the 30th ASEAN Summit, he also recalled the principles of the group's founding fathers, emphasising the mutual respect for independence, sovereignty, equality, territorial integrity, national identity, and non-interference (Duterte, 2017a). However, Duterte's nationalist rhetoric acquires its particular flavour through frequent references to the realities of ordinary people rather than a more abstract 'national interest'. He claimed that a central goal of ASEAN should be to 'empower' the peoples of its member-states and to cultivate 'ownership' of the organisation among them (ABS-CBN News, 2019; ERIA, 2017). He thus frames the relation between national interests and regional cooperation in terms of popular sovereignty, in the sense that regional organisations should serve all member-states' citizens as their ultimate constituency. This framing resonates well with ASEAN's discourse of building a 'people-centred' or 'people-oriented' community.

The same people-oriented definition of the national interest can be seen in Duterte's shift from the United States to China. When asked if he would push for bilateral talks with China, Duterte replied: 'We have this pact with the West, but I want everybody to know that we will be charting a course of our own. .... It will not be dependent on America. And it will be a line that is not intended to please anybody but the Filipino interest' (quoted in Baviera, 2016: 206). Whereas the United States is perceived as a hegemonic and colonial power that constrains the interests of the nation, Duterte frames cooperation with China in terms of establishing independence from any single major power, with the aim of reorienting the country's foreign relations through a people-to-people approach to benefit national interests and ordinary Filipinos (Arugay, 2018). To prevent rapprochement with China from stoking popular nationalism, the government presents cooperation with Beijing not primarily as part of a broader geopolitical strategy but as a way to improve the lives of ordinary Filipinos, for example, the country's fishermen (Baviera & Pante, 2019: 118).

6.2 Institutional Preferences

Duterte's framings of regional cooperation identify the United States as the main embodiment of a liberal elite, against which he positions the Philippine people alongside their regional neighbours. Following a populist strategy, he portrays himself as the leader taking back control from foreign, corrupt domination. Accordingly, his institutional preferences mirror those of fellow populists like Orbán and Chávez.

6.2.1 Regional Summitry and State Visits

By making use of the summit structures in ASEAN's intergovernmental design and resorting to bilateral talks with China whenever needed, Duterte is able to maximise his freedom to act and pursue his strategic goals. As a loosely structured executive-driven organisation, ASEAN can change its agenda frequently according to the national preferences of the chairpersonship of any given year (Tay, 2017: 49). During his 2017 chairpersonship of ASEAN, Duterte steered the agenda of the organisation towards his strategic preferences, such as his domestic war on drugs (Sevilla, 2018: 165). Likewise, Baviera and Pante (2019: 119) point out how Duterte used his position as chairperson to promote Filipino interests through ASEAN–China relations and the ASEAN–China dialogue. He also advanced leader-driven cooperation bilaterally. Between taking office in June 2016 and August 2019, he had concluded five visits to China and had met no less than eight times with Chinese President Xi Jinping (Calonzo, 2019). This summit diplomacy fits into his transactional notion of foreign policy as a matter of cunning statecraft, which stands in marked contrast to the Philippines' traditional strategy of pursuing principled integration in the US-led LIO (Heydarian, 2017: 220, 2018: 58–71).

However, Duterte does not rely exclusively on ASEAN in his regional foreign policy. By engaging in a variety of other regional institutions, such as the Chinese-driven Asian Infrastructure Investment Bank (AIIB) and the Japanese-dominated Asian Development Bank (ADB), Duterte avoided leaning too much on one particular organisation, which would have restrained his authority and steering capacity. Clearly, Duterte's personal preferences matter a great deal for any attempt to uncover the patterns of Philippine foreign policy under his mandate. This becomes particularly evident in the way he dealt with the South China Sea issue – by radically departing from the country's traditional approach and building 'warmer relations' with China (Duterte, 2017c). In the 2019 State of the Nation address, Duterte openly declared his sympathies with President Xi Jinping ('we just became friends') and explained why his administration would not expel China from Philippine waters (Duterte, 2019b). While engaging with ASEAN, Duterte is aware that the bloc's consensus-style decision-making limits his ability to steer the organisation according to his own strategic interests. Cooperation with China on issues like the Belt and Road

Initiative (BRI) can balance out a lack of progress within ASEAN. In this, he follows a general pattern among ASEAN states, which often weigh their commitment to ASEAN frameworks against bilateral options (Huong, 2018: 14).

6.2.2 Rituals and Trouble-Maker Diplomacy

To contribute to the legitimation of his government both domestically and internationally, Duterte has employed an unorthodox diplomatic style and symbolic performances to enact his populist strategy on a regional level. He seems to regard ASEAN as a strategic space in which to promote his own domestic political agenda, legitimise his regime in the eyes of his people, and defend himself against his critics. The organisation's summit events provide him with a stage on which to project his image as an outsider in the diplomatic community, along with his unorthodox views on international relations (Arugay, 2018: 5). These summits, as well as the numerous high-level (Track II) policy dialogues that form an integral part of ASEAN regionalism, take on a strong symbolic meaning. Peterson and Maiquez (2020: 36) succinctly summarise this symbolic value of ASEAN meetings: 'Events and performances in the gathering provide a fascinating case study into the ways in which theatre and performance in the service of politics can serve the needs of a host government while reflecting an aspirational ASEAN identity, one rooted in a mythic past and reflective of its archipelagic nature as a geopolitical, economic, and historical construct.' ASEAN provides its leaders not just with public spaces but also with a rich repertoire of symbols and rituals conveying a sense of regional solidarity, like flags, banners, slogans, handshakes, photo ops, and so on (see Davies, 2018). Duterte has used these abundantly to legitimate himself vis-à-vis domestic and international audiences. The ceremonies surrounding the ASEAN Summit in Manila during the Philippine chairpersonship in 2017 are the most vivid example. The theatrical performances celebrating the organisation's fiftieth anniversary at that meeting ostensibly invoked a pan-ASEAN identity but were carefully choreographed to portray Duterte as a strongman navigating his country through the global forces of neoliberalism (Peterson & Maiquez, 2020: 52). Amplifying his populist message, he also used the slogan of a 'people-centred ASEAN' to demand that the organisation's policies be more responsive to the interests of the people (Duterte, 2016a).

Duterte's use of derogatory language to delegitimate leaders and institutions of the LIO exemplifies a foreign policy embellished with populist performances (Arugay, 2018: 2). Especially during the ASEAN chairpersonship at the organisation's fiftieth anniversary, Duterte displayed his extreme and unorthodox diplomatic style (Arugay, 2018), enacting his role as an authentic 'man of the people'. Another example was when his use of insulting language towards US President Barack Obama sparked diplomatic outrage ahead of the ASEAN Summit meetings in September 2016 and led to the cancellation of a bilateral meeting between the two heads of state (Rappler, 2016). At the East Asia Summit just days after those remarks, Duterte digressed from his prepared script to invoke a colonial-era massacre of Muslim Filipinos by US soldiers (Agence France-Press, 2016). Framing US brutality in the Philippines as crimes against his own ancestors, this unusual move was supposed to expose the hypocrisy behind the US government's concerns for human rights violations committed by his administration (Heydarian, 2018: 46).

6.2.3 Regionalising the Domestic Agenda

Despite Duterte's use of regional cooperation for symbolic performances, he pursues concrete policy output on certain selected issues that connect to his domestic political agenda. The strategic use of ASEAN to legitimise his controversial war on drugs at home and abroad is among the most telling aspects of Duterte's understanding of populist regionalism. For example, during the Philippine ASEAN chairpersonship in 2017, the undersecretary for policy of the Department of Foreign Affairs, Enrique Austria Manalo, declared that the first point in the new agenda would be 'strengthening cooperation in combating and preventing the use of dangerous and illicit drugs' (Manalo, 2017). Duterte used a similar rhetoric in several interventions between 2016 and 2019 (Adel, 2019). During these summits, as well as on many other occasions, Duterte promoted some of his own interests, such as stronger collaboration in combating drugs and crimes as well as an agreement on a code of conduct in the South China Sea that would bolster improved relations with China (Jennings, 2017). In fact, these issues are directly connected, as the rapprochement with China has been interpreted as a move to secure Beijing's support for his anti-drug campaign (Destradi & Plagemann, 2019: 16). Duterte has also pushed ASEAN to finalise the Regional Comprehensive Economic Partnership (RCEP), a China-backed trade agreement, while criticising the US-led Trans-Pacific Partnership (TPP) – a move that 'can be taken as a significant step in the Philippines' pursuit of an independent foreign policy, which greatly revolves around its "strategic shift" away from the U.S. and towards China' (Katigbak, 2017: 2).

While the United States – mostly during the Obama administration – was quite vociferous in its criticism of Duterte's ruthless war on drugs, China was always quite supportive of it, both rhetorically and financially (Arugay, 2018; De Castro, 2018, 2019; Heydarian, 2018; Palanca & Ong, 2018). Duterte seems to flexibly adapt his strategies of engagement in line with domestic legitimation strategies: he has 'symbolically' departed from the United States, pragmatically approached China, and resorted to ASEAN when necessary. Despite the harsh rhetoric, Duterte never intended to fully abandon the Philippines' traditional US ally (Baviera, 2016) but rather aimed at maximising his options by strategically engaging with different partners (Sevilla, 2018).

7 Comparison: Identifying a Populist Script of Regional Cooperation

The three case studies confirm our expectations about the regional cooperation strategies of populist leaders. While there are clearly some important differences, which can be explained in part by the respective leaders' ideological leanings, the core political logic of populism leads them to make sense of regional cooperation through the common lens of the people–elite antagonism. This serves as a meta-frame that shapes all six dimensions of the analytical framework. This section compares the findings of the three case studies and teases out the commonalities in the framings and institutional preferences, which can be seen as constituent features of an emerging populist script of regional cooperation.

7.1 Populist Framings of Regional Cooperation

Anti-Liberalism.   When populist governments engage in regional cooperation, they seem to do so to contest or reject specific aspects of the LIO. Their challenges are usually formulated in opposition to certain actors that are seen as hegemonic representatives of that order. Chávez's socialist brand of populism mainly targeted the LIO's economic dimensions. It rejected the neoliberal agenda of the global trade and financial regime embodied by the United States and the Bretton Woods institutions. Orbán and Duterte, by contrast, focus on political norms and institutions. Duterte's framing in particular refutes liberal cosmopolitanism in the sense of a perceived imposition of a universalist human rights agenda by Western actors and the UN. Orbán positions Hungary as a model for 'illiberal' democracy against the pluralist values and supranational institutions promoted by EU institutions and the Western European states whose interests they ostensibly represent. For Duterte and Chávez, Western hegemony in the LIO's institutional dimension is (was) an additional trigger for contestation, which is why they deploy(ed) anti-imperialist or anti-colonialist rhetoric and challenge(d) global governance institutions as instruments of US or Western interests. While these findings confirm existing research on the differences between right-wing and left-wing populism, they also highlight anti-liberalism and challenges to hegemonic representatives of the LIO as the common denominator of populist framings of regional cooperation.

Multiple and Threatened Identity.   Identity politics is an ever-present feature of populist strategies. The leaders' appeals to shared values, history, and culture play a major role in framing regional cooperation. Contrary to conventional wisdom, the analysis shows that populist governments not only are able to reconcile national identity with the construction of a regional identity but even actively promote the latter for the dual purpose of bolstering their own domestic political strategies and enabling mutual legitimation among fellow populist governments. Regional identity is often constructed on notions of a struggle against a common threat or mutual enemy, usually the representative of the LIO identified in the respective anti-liberal framing. While populist leaders do not necessarily perceive regional cooperation in terms of bloc-like alliances, their idea of regionalism is one where the members of regional organisations mutually legitimate one another, in particular by refraining from critique or intervention, even when a member violates well-established international norms. Chávez used ALBA extensively to invoke a shared identity under the banner of *Nuestramérica* as a basis for solidarity with other Latin American regimes that were criticised by Western governments and international organisations. Similar claims for anti-liberal solidarity against Western intervention are made by Duterte, who calls for unity among ASEAN 'friends, brothers, and sisters' and insists on the organisation's norm of non-intervention to fend off criticism of human rights violations. But populists can also tap into other sources of common identity, such as religious ties in the case of Orbán's invocation of Christianity as a basis for 'Central Europeanness' in the V4 states. All of these constructions aim to portray the people as a morally pure – but in fact not homogeneous – collective constituency of the leaders' regional cooperation initiatives.

Popular Sovereignty.   Although all three populist governments draw to some extent on nationalist rhetoric, there is no evidence this translates into unilateral and inward-oriented foreign policy stances. On the contrary, regional cooperation is framed as a way of re-establishing sovereignty over the elite-driven LIO. Populist governments tend to endorse and actively engage in regional cooperation when it promises to enhance, rather than threaten, sovereignty. As suggested by previous research, cooperation thus appears as a means to legitimate populists' hold on power. Beyond boosting national prestige through international recognition, however, the empirical findings demonstrate that populists frame and justify regional cooperation specifically in terms of *popular* sovereignty. They ascribe a major value to it insofar as it supports their mission of linking politics to the will of the people. An important common theme is that cooperation should preserve the autonomy and independence of the populist leader to pursue policies on behalf of the people, free from external domination – be that from the Brussels elite in the case of Orbán, neoliberal hegemony in the case of Chávez, or Western interference and paternalism in the case of Duterte. More often than outright rejections of regional organisations, we find demands that such organisations should serve their popular constituencies and improve the everyday lives of the ordinary citizens in their respective member-states (e.g. Europe as the 'home of nations', *Nuestramérica* as a Latin American homeland, and a 'people-centred' ASEAN).

7.2 Institutional Preferences

Leader-Driven Formats. With regard to the institutional preferences that derive from these framings, the three populist leaders maintain a preference for regional institutions that are loosely structured by design and give extensive discretion to heads of state. Both Orbán's promotion of the V4 as a 'concert of sovereign nations' and the 'presidential regionalism' pursued by Chávez through ALBA and CELAC are cases in point. When it comes to existing institutions, the leaders selectively engage in formats that best represent this preference or push for institutional reforms – as in the case of Orbán's demand to strengthen the inter-governmental character of the EU. In addition, there is a strong aspiration among all three populist governments to acquire a leading role within selected settings. They have tried to boost their own role within some regional organisations (V4 for Orbán, ALBA/CELAC for Chávez, and ASEAN for Duterte), and they have in many cases contested those in which they have felt marginalised (the EU for Orbán, the FTAA and the OAS for Chávez). They have used their leadership to steer regionalism towards serving their specific goals and purposes, either by convincing their fellow regional partners of the general benefits of certain initiatives or by implicitly forcing them to support their agenda. When they fail to exert influence, they may react by forum shopping, as Chávez's turn from the CAN and the G-3 to Mercosur and UNASUR or Duterte's oscillating between regional engagement with ASEAN and bilateral diplomatic overtures towards China demonstrate. Populist leaders favour leader-driven regional institutions and organisations for two important reasons. First, centralised and supranational regional institutions constrain, control, or regulate state behaviour, which sits uneasily with attempts to frame regionalism in terms of popular sovereignty. Second, leader-driven institutions provide populist leaders with opportunities to present themselves as the front figures of regional organisations (as in Latin America's 'presidential-led' regionalism), which serves their domestic self-legitimation.

Symbolism.   The preference for leader-driven formats is linked to the strong discursive and symbolic elements of contemporary populism. The empirical analysis shows that populists generally use regional cooperation for performative purposes. Grandiose rhetoric contrasts with limited practical implications in terms of joint problem-solving and policy implementation. There is a pattern of populist leaders praising the goals of regional organisations, signing cooperation treaties, and taking part in 'summitry regionalism'. For them, a central purpose of regional organisations is to contribute to the domestic legitimation of their member-state governments by pooling symbolic and discursive power, demonstrating mutual support, and asserting their formal sovereignty and international status. Chávez's speeches at ALBA meetings were infused with militaristic language ('homeland or death') and references to protagonists of national liberation such as Simón Bolívar to legitimate the leaders of the organisation's member-states as modern-day reincarnations of anti-colonial heroes. Symbolic legitimation by means of regional cooperation is particularly important for populist leaders facing external criticism for authoritarian tendencies, which is or was the case for all three leaders in the analysis. The three leaders have also used the publicity of regional meetings to increase the reach of their unorthodox communication styles and to break with diplomatic conventions, be that by drawing heavily on social media, as in the case of Orbán, or by using profane language, as in the case of Duterte, who famously used abrasive language against US President Obama on the sidelines of an ASEAN Summit in 2016. These enactments of a maverick identity help leaders maintain their image as representatives of the authentic people against a detached elite. Regional organisations thus serve more as brands, symbols, and spaces for performances, while their authority to bind members to implement collective action is seen as secondary or even counterproductive.

À la Carte **Cooperation.**   Finally, the comparative analysis reveals that populist governments generally seem to favour a cherry-picking or *à la carte* approach to regional cooperation. In spite of broad formal and symbolic commitments, most populist governments will ultimately follow through with regional cooperation only in areas that they perceive as serving their own political strategy. While populists are eager to signal their dedication to regional cooperation on a broad range of issues, such commitments are usually symbolic and detached from actual implementation efforts. By contrast, for those selected policy fields prioritised according to domestic purposes, populists actually expect regional organisations to deliver in terms of problem-solving. Duterte used the Philippine chairperson-ship of ASEAN to push the fight against illegal drugs – the driving force behind his popular support – to the top of the organisation's agenda. Orbán began to heavily lobby for restrictive asylum policies and strengthened border controls in the EU once the so-called refugee crisis became his main source of domestic mobilisation and legitimation. Chávez, meanwhile, was able to showcase cooperation projects focused on social policy and development for the poor as evidence that transnational socialist solidarity translates into benefits for the ordinary people. In all of these cases, functional cooperation demands alone cannot explain the sometimes extreme prioritisation of some issue areas over others, and especially the readiness to sacrifice cooperation gains in other fields. Duterte, for example, was so eager in prioritising his search for material support in his war on drugs over other issues that he overturned his initially antagonistic stance towards Chinese advances in the South China Sea, essentially crushing years of ASEAN efforts to maintain a unitary stance on the issue. Despite the principled, Manichean foundations of populist strategy, populist foreign policies thus display a highly pragmatic and opportunistic drive when it comes to regional cooperation.

7.3 Summary

Overall, the comparison provides clear evidence of a populist script of regional cooperation. Obviously, foreign policies as a whole are influenced by a myriad of factors and not reducible to populism. It does not come as a surprise, therefore, that the cooperation strategies of populist leaders differ considerably across cases. However, our engagement with theories of populism has enabled us to distil common patterns that are clearly attributable to leaders' populist strategies. Table 1 displays the general components of this script, as well as how they manifest concretely in the individual cases. Populist strategies of regional cooperation rely on anti-liberal, identity-based, and pro-sovereignty framings of regionalism. In terms of institutional preferences, they favour leader-driven regionalism at the expense of regional bureaucracies and supranational institutions. This is closely connected to the prioritisation of symbolic cooperation over effective implementation, and *à la carte* strategies in terms of concrete cooperation. The existence of the script drives home the argument that despite the emphasis on different variants of populism in the recent scholarship, the concept of 'populism' as such has analytical value for researchers of regional cooperation, as well as International Relations more broadly.

It bears repeating that our findings do not imply that regional organisations are necessarily becoming more populist per se in terms of their policies and institutional design. However, our study definitively shows that the populist script has already left its mark on debates about institutional change and policy reform in several regional organisations. It therefore becomes imperative to

Table 1 Comparison of frames and institutional preferences of Orbán, Chávez, and Duterte

	Orbán	Chávez	Duterte
Anti-liberalism	Illiberal democracy Vs political liberalism, represented by Western Europe and its liberal ideas of democracy and good governance	Anti-imperialism and anti-hegemonism Vs economic liberalism and liberal internationalism, represented by the United States and the Bretton Woods institutions with their neocolonial and neoliberal agenda	Anti-cosmopolitanism Vs political liberalism and liberal internationalism, represented by the United States and the UN with their criticism of the war on drugs based on universalist human rights ideas
Multiple (and threatened) identity	European and Christian identity 'Central Europeanness', solidarity against threat to moral pureness of the people	*Nuestramérica* Latin American community, solidarity against threat of imperialist and expansionist North America	Filipino nationalism and the 'ASEAN family' 'ASEAN centrality', unity and solidarity against threat of external (Western) intervention Chinese identity People-oriented community
Popular sovereignty	Europe as the 'home of nations' Cooperation to re-establish national sovereignty vs disenfranchisement by EU-style postnational supranationalism	Regionalism for the peoples of Latin America Cooperation to preserve fought-for independence against neocolonial forces, to achieve equal distribution of cooperation benefits to all social groups	Cooperation to preserve autonomy despite great power influence and to empower the peoples of ASEAN member-states

Leader-driven formats	V4 as a 'concert of sovereign states' Push for reform of EU: 'strong EU relies on strong member-states'	'Inter-presidential' organisations Forum shopping (ALBA, Mercosur, UNASUR, CELAC) to increase influence	Making use of ASEAN's intergovernmental structures State visits Forum shopping and playing China against ASEAN to maximise freedom of action
Symbolic cooperation	V4 summitry Joint speeches and awards among like-minded leaders	ALBA summitry Militaristic and revolutionary rhetoric, metaphorical language, and references to anti-colonial heroes	ASEAN symbols and rituals Promotion of 'people-centred' ASEAN Unorthodox diplomatic style
À la carte	Migration agenda within EU V4 Defence Cooperation	Development cooperation aimed at the poor (health, education) Energy and financial independence	War on drugs South China Sea issue Regional economic cooperation

discuss the implications of these developments for the LIO – an issue to which we turn in the next section.

8 Implications for Research on the Contestation of the LIO

Our comparative study of populist framings and institutional preferences regarding regional cooperation highlights the importance of domestic politics as a main driver behind the increasing contestation of the LIO. The strikingly similar patterns of cooperation frames across the three cases suggest that contestation of the LIO is not determined by conventional binaries dominating the previous literature, such as the North–South divide (or 'West versus the Rest'), liberals versus non-liberals, losers versus winners of globalisation, or right-wing versus left-wing populism. As a generic strategy for maintaining governmental power, populism is available to leaders across different ideologies and structural positions in world politics, and it seems that contesting the LIO is a core feature of this strategy. Of course, more systematic research on the different variations of populist contestation is needed in the future, especially beyond the heavy focus on right-wing populists in the West (Destradi & Plagemann, 2019). However, we highlight three ways in which our findings contribute to theory building as well as a more nuanced intellectual debate around the contestation of the LIO: (i) thinking beyond the LIO, (ii) exploring populist legitimation and delegitimation in global governance, and (iii) problematising the liberal–populist divide.

8.1 Thinking Beyond the LIO

Most of the literature about the demise and contestations of the LIO – especially works emanating from within its Western core – is implicitly or explicitly normatively biased in favour of liberal norms and ideas. For many scholars, the LIO is inherently 'good' and more or less synonymous with international order per se (Colgan & Keohane, 2017; Ikenberry, 2011). Contestation is therefore viewed *ex negativo* – that is, with regard to how it threatens that order – instead of in terms of the substantial alternatives it offers. From this point of view, contestation promises chaos, and the antidote to that threat is to reinforce the liberal order, be that by means of renewed US leadership or socialising and co-opting contenders into existing norms and institutions (see Ikenberry, 2011, 2018a, 2018b; Slaughter, 2017). Scholars such as Acharya (2018) and Stuenkel (2016) have rightfully criticised this Western-centric view because it underestimates the political traction that alternative visions for international order have gained in different parts of the world. We agree with these authors that future research and political debates must avoid getting trapped in the false choice between liberal order and disorder and instead look at the alternative conceptions of order that contestants from the Global South as well as many groups outside the political establishment in the North carry.

Our exploration of a populist script of international cooperation demonstrates clearly that the populist wave does not herald the end of international collaboration, as is often implied. On the contrary, new discourses and strategies of international and regional cooperation are forming in which populist leaders actively endorse certain forms of international and regional cooperation. Contestation based on the populist script does not automatically translate into unilateralism. While organisations associated with the LIO (such as the WTO and the EU) are often contested, populists engage in counter-institutionalisation (Zürn, 2018: 170–94) by strengthening new and non-liberal regional organisations (such as the V4 and ALBA). But even as criticism of the institutions of the LIO is a hallmark of populist rhetoric, all case studies included in this Element reveal that populist leaders continue to be active and collaborate even within the dominant regional international organisations (EU, Mercosur, ASEAN). In this sense, our study of populist leaders differs quite sharply from the baseline assumption permeating most of the literature on the LIO and international organisations. Our focus on populism as a political strategy explains this seeming paradox by pointing to the international stage for symbolic performances provided by these institutions, leaders' claims to reassert popular sovereignty over them, and their *à la carte* instrumentalisation for domestic purposes. This also explains the attempts – often coordinated – to transform organisational cultures and designs in line with the frames and preferences of the populist script, for example by shifting power from technocrats and supranational institutions to more leader-driven decision-making and relying on ceremonial meetings. Populists' relation to the LIO is thus characterised by a mix of different and sometimes contradictory strategies, including discursive rejection, but also counter-institutionalisation and pressure for reform from within the organisational frameworks of the LIO. Although these strategies may sometimes seem erratic or rejectionist, they are shaped by an overarching strategy that contains distinct judgements about, and alternatives for, the LIO.

8.2 Populist Legitimation and Delegitimation in Global Governance

Populist contestation is inextricably linked to the legitimacy of international order (Tallberg & Zürn, 2019; Zürn, 2004, 2018). According to Ikenberry (2018a: 19), 'the crisis of the liberal order is a crisis of legitimacy and social purpose.' However, populism should not be understood as a mere reaction to an *a priori* existing lack of legitimacy of global governance institutions, which would be to underestimate the agency of populist leaders in actively shaping legitimacy perceptions of the LIO. As a political strategy, populism offers a rather powerful toolbox for purposefully delegitimating the LIO through specific frames. While the literature has theorised different objects and processes of legitimation, our study offers insights into specifically populist ways of legitimating and delegitimating global and regional governance institutions, and how these processes interact with populists' domestic self-legitimation strategies. More to the point, the three frames we identify as core components of the populist script sidestep discussions about whether global governance institutions are effective and legitimate with regard to input and output legitimacy, hitherto the most commonly accepted categories of legitimacy in global governance. Instead, populists' domestic political interests and their goal of reinforcing the idea of an elite–citizen gap in global governance institutions (see Dellmuth et al., 2019) lead them to invoke a more principled opposition based on notions of identity and sovereignty. From this perspective, the liberal emphasis on public goods and functional problem-solving remains secondary for populist leaders.

Populist delegitimation strategies are much more difficult to address than contestation focusing on performance and procedural aspects. Because their calculation of cooperation gains and sovereignty costs follows a rationale that differs from that assumed by liberal integration theories (see Section 3.3), institutional reforms aimed at increasing the effectiveness or inclusiveness of regional and global governance are unlikely to impress populist leaders. Enhanced capacities for functional problem-solving or increasing transparency and accountability do not (at least not in themselves) offset the identitarian and sovereigntist logic of populist legitimation and delegitimation. For example, the further enhancement of the European Parliament's competences would do nothing to prevent populist anti-EU contestation from Orbán, because he frames the very idea of transnational representation and legislation as undermining popular sovereignty. The mismatch between the reliance on conventional legitimation frames by established stakeholders of the LIO and the resonance of populist frames among key audiences is vital to understanding the current legitimacy crisis of the LIO.

Our study suggests new avenues of research in this regard. Existing research on legitimacy remains heavily centred on legitimacy beliefs rooted in liberal norms and functional problem-solving and is therefore unable to capture the content and resonance of populist (de)legitimation strategies. We propose that future research can explore (i) the sources and norms on which populists draw to challenge established (largely liberal) multilateral institutions and (ii) the sources and norms on which populists draw to justify alternative institutions, especially regional organisations. Without providing ready answers, we suspect that communitarian and structural theories of International Relations may prove to be more helpful in this regard than the varieties of liberal-institutionalist theories that currently dominate the study of legitimacy in global governance (see Tallberg & Zürn, 2019). What we can say for sure is that any theoretical approach would need to pay close attention to the domestic level, since it is there that we find the main sources of populist (de)legitimation strategies on the international level.

8.3 Problematising the Liberal–Populist Divide

To a great extent, the populist script is developing in an explicit rejection of the LIO. Scholars are therefore correct to argue that the populist wave brings with it an increased polarisation of world politics. However, we argue that it would be wrong to conceptualise the division between populism and liberalism as the defining new fault line of international society. Populists, especially in liberal electoral regimes, rely on continued popular support. This makes for volatile and ever-shifting alignments, rather than the clear demarcation between a liberal and a populist camp suggested by the existing literature. Just think of the possibilities for a common populist strategy in the EU before and after the unforeseen collapse of government coalitions including the Freedom Party of Austria (FPÖ) and the Lega Nord in Italy within just a few weeks of each other. Moreover, the very notion of populism as a strategy implies that even nominally 'liberal' governments can occasionally draw on populist logics to build support. For example, analysts have shown that the leadership of French President Emmanuel Macron, a self-styled defender of the LIO and a vocal opponent of populist parties, displays clear populist traits itself. In the 2017 presidential election, for example, Macron ran on an anti-elitist campaign promising a renewal of the political class based on a common French heritage (Fougère & Barthold, 2020). In an important sense, then, reifying the rift between populist and non-populist actors as a matter of essential identities is creating a false dichotomy. In our view, unpacking the liberal–populist divide is not equivalent to exaggerated normative relativism but rather a step towards a better understanding of the complexities of the contestation of the LIO.

The conventional liberal–populist binary can also be problematised with regard to traditional liberal ideals. Even if populist leaders usually endorse forms of regional cooperation that protect their national room for manoeuvre, boost their status as national leaders, and advance their domestic populist strategies, they are by no means always opposed to functional problem-solving and cooperation for mutual gains, as emphasised in liberal thinking.

In fact, in several policy fields we are witnessing mutual accommodation and cooperation across the liberal–populist divide. In particular, the *à la carte* approach that we identify as a crucial feature of populists' cooperation preferences creates opportunities under conditions of coinciding interests. After all, issues such as migration, drugs, health, and security are not populist per se. The fact that populists rely on 'results', 'efficiency', and the achievement of public goods to showcase their success to their domestic constituencies creates possibilities for tying (and potentially constraining) populist leaders into institutionalised cooperation in certain policy fields. Some populist leaders have even positioned themselves in support of the Paris Agreement, including notably Orbán, who argued that 'action against climate change requires action at a global level' (quoted in Schaller & Carius, 2019: 22). The member-states of Orbán's V4 have also been champions of closer defence cooperation in the EU. This is by no means equivalent to saying that any kind of cooperation is desirable from a normative point of view, and cooperation with populists clearly involves risks for mainstream politicians. Indeed, the concessions made by liberal EU members in response to anti-migration sentiments stoked by populist challengers such as Orbán show that bridges between liberals and populists can easily be constructed on the backs of already marginalised groups. Although cooperation between governments relying on populist strategies and proponents of the LIO is likely to be *ad hoc* – depending on the whims of domestic politics rather than expressing long-standing strategic partnerships – our contribution offers a more nuanced counterpoint to the dominant narrative of impending conflict.

9 Conclusion

This Element investigates populist leaders' strategies for regional cooperation. We draw on theoretical approaches to the domestic logic of populist politics and an extensive comparative case study to argue that populist leaders make sense of regional cooperation using three frames: anti-liberalism, multilayered and threatened identity, and popular sovereignty. On the basis of these framings, populist leaders adopt institutional preferences that favour leader-driven, symbolic, and *à la carte* forms of cooperation. By no means do we intend to claim that populist governments will always promote regional cooperation. Neither do we claim that populist regional cooperation is necessarily desirable from a normative standpoint. Our argument is rather that insofar as populists engage in regionalism, they are likely to see it through the lens of these frames and try to reshape regional cooperation mechanisms in line with these institutional preferences.

While it would be premature to diagnose populist regionalism as a uniform type of cooperation, the remarkable degree of coherence in how different populist governments view regional cooperation suggests that a populist script of regional cooperation is emerging. In particular, this populist script challenges the LIO with regard to the latter's emphasis on delegation and pooling of sovereignty, as well as its focus on achieving public goods and good governance as the main purpose of regional cooperation. By contrast, populist regionalism aims at preserving governmental autonomy and re-establishing popular sovereignty against liberal elites. The findings confirm the conventional wisdom that populist governments' appeals to shared values, history, and culture inform their political strategies, and that they thrive on contesting some or all dimensions of the LIO (i.e. political liberalism, economic liberalism, and liberal internationalism) (see Börzel & Risse, 2019). However, populism does not necessarily lead to unilateral nationalism. Insofar as populist leaders deploy nationalist rhetoric, they usually reconcile it with regional identities to legitimate certain types of regional cooperation. In other words, populist governments tend to endorse and be active partners in regional cooperation as long as it does not endanger popular sovereignty and their rather narrow understanding of national identity.

By conceptualising populism as a political strategy, our study contributes to current debates on the contestation of the LIO. Whereas most approaches in the debate around the LIO treat states as black boxes or focus on popular grievances, we bring domestic politics into the analysis to uncover the crucial role that political leaders' strategies play in the translation of individual grievances into contestation of international norms and institutions. This theoretical angle opens new theoretically and empirically grounded perspectives on ongoing questions regarding the role of domestic politics in contestation of the LIO, alternatives to liberal conceptions of order, the role of populism in legitimation and delegitimation of regional and global governance, and the need to problematise the liberal–populist divide. Specifically, the study reveals that populist leaders prefer loosely structured regional institutions that provide considerable room to manoeuvre for themselves and their governments – an approach that is at odds with the liberal script of institutionalised and intrusive authority (Börzel & Zürn, 2021). While populist leaders explicitly challenge and resist established and heavily institutionalised organisations, they endorse those that provide them with opportunities to present themselves as representatives of 'the people' vs 'the elite'. Hence, they seek to instrumentalise regional organisations in line with populist frames and institutional preferences. At the same time, however, populists sometimes strive for tangible results and problem-solving cooperation in areas that drive their domestic strategies. This tension between radicalism and pragmatism opens opportunities for effective governance and problem-solving in specific policy fields, but it also forges normative questions. To the extent that liberal policymakers would find it expedient to cooperate with populists, one of the main challenges is to find common solutions that offset the exclusionary impulse that often accompanies populist ideologies.

One important question that demands further investigation relates to the generalisability of the populist script of regional cooperation. What about the isolationist tendencies of Trumpism and Brexit? What about leaders who, like Narendra Modi in India, eschew regional initiatives? It is important to recognise that the existence of populist leaders without a predisposition towards regional cooperation does not put the populist script in doubt, but it reminds us that the script offers a *potential* way of legitimating regional cooperation in a way that resonates with the populist political logic. The populist script does not dictate a particular foreign policy stance. Looking at Boris Johnson, Narendra Modi, and Donald Trump gives us some indications regarding what may be countervailing conditions for the pursuit of regional cooperation in accordance with the populist script. While more systematic research is needed on this question, we propose four tentative hypotheses. Not all of them may apply equally across the three cases, but each may have some explanatory power for at least one of them.

First, the size or status of the United Kingdom, India and the United States as major powers may play a role and set their leaders apart from populists in more average-size states. To take a cue from realist thinking, unilateral or isolationist foreign policy stances may be more easily available or seem strategically more promising to governments of states with ample resources than to those of smaller ones. By contrast, pooling capabilities within regional organisations may be a sound choice for small and medium-sized states. A second potential factor is the absence of political allies in geographical proximity. While Donald Trump's neighbour Mexican President Andrés Manuel López Obrador arguably draws on a populist strategy, his more left-leaning politics and clashes over issues like the wall on the Mexico–United States border make him an unlikely candidate for regional collaboration. A similar constellation can be found in South Asia, where India's neighbour Pakistan is led by populist Imran Khan, but the animosities between the two states have prevented functioning regional cooperation. Third, in states where there is a broad and deeply entrenched anti-regionalist political discourse, as in the United Kingdom, populist leaders may need to adopt more extreme positions to 'one-up' their political opponents. In a country of Eurosceptics, radical opposition to the integration project may become the only way of standing out as an anti-elite candidate. A final point relates to the institutional context: especially in South Asia, regional organisations like the South Asian Association for Regional Cooperation (SAARC) have been perceived as weak and more or less irrelevant. Under these circumstances, it may be risky or counterproductive for populist leaders to make regional cooperation a cornerstone of their foreign policy, as it cannot easily be framed as a countermeasure against an elite-dominated project of disenfranchising the people. Precisely because of their largely inconsequential image, it is hard to frame organisations like SAARC as dark forces against which the people have to be defended through regional cooperation among the champions of popular sovereignty.

Abbreviations

ADB	Asian Development Bank
AIIB	Asian Infrastructure Investment Bank
ALBA	Bolivarian Alliance for the Peoples of Our America
BRI	Belt and Road Initiative
CAN	Andean Community
CELAC	Community of Latin American and Caribbean States
EU	European Union
FKGP	Independent Smallholders' Party
FPÖ	Freedom Party of Austria
FTAA	Free Trade Area of the Americas
G-3	Grupo de los Tres
IMF	International Monetary Fund
LIO	Liberal International Order
MDF	Hungarian Democratic Forum
Mercosur	Southern Common Market
NATO	North Atlantic Treaty Organization
OAS	Organization of American States
OECD	Organisation for Economic Co-operation and Development
RCEP	Regional Comprehensive Economic Partnership
SAARC	South Asian Association for Regional Cooperation
TCP	People's Trade Agreement
TPP	Trans-Pacific Partnership
UN	United Nations
UNASUR	Union of South American Nations
V4	Visegrád Group
WTO	World Trade Organization

References

ABS-CBN News (2017). ANC Live: Duterte blasts UN, EU anew, dares envoys to leave PH 'in 24 hrs'. *Youtube*, 12 October [Video]. Retrieved from www.youtube.com/watch?v=Y-jrWQSdOEA

ABS-CBN News (2019). Duterte: ASEAN needs to invest more on people. 23 June. Retrieved from https://news.abs-cbn.com/overseas/06/23/19/duterte-asean-needs-to-assert-role-at-evolving-regional-architecture.

About Hungary (2018). PM Orbán pledges to govern 'a sovereign Hungarian state of free Hungarians'. 11 May. Retrieved from http://abouthungary.hu/news-in-brief/pm-orban-pledges-to-govern-a-sovereign-hungarian-state-of-free-hungarians/

Acharya, A. (2018). *The End of American World Order*, 2nd edn. Cambridge: Polity Press.

Adel, R. (2019). Duterte urges ASEAN anew: Redouble collective efforts vs drugs, other threats. *PhilStar*, 23 June. Retrieved from www.philstar.com/headlines/2019/06/23/1928887/duterte-urges-asean-anew-redouble-collective-efforts-vs-drugs-other-threats

Agence France-Presse (2016). Obama, Duterte clash over brutal crime war. *Rappler.com*, 8 September. Retrieved from www.rappler.com/nation/145656-duterte-obama-clash-crime-drug-war

Alaniz, M. (2013). La política de Hugo Chávez y la prensa venezolana (2005–2006). *Debates Urgentes*, 2(3), 131–56.

ALBA (2008). Declaración de Solidaridad y Apoyo a la República de Bolivia. 23 April. Retrieved from www.lavozdelsandinismo.com/internacionales/2008-04-24/respalda-cumbre-del-alba-al-gobierno-constitucional-de-bolivia/

ALBA (2009). Declaración de la VII Cumbre del ALBA-TCP. 17 October. Retrieved from www.fidelcastro.cu/en/node/26655

Altmann-Borbón, J. (2019). ALBA before its greatest challenge: Survive. *World Government Research Network*, 2 November. Retrieved from https://2bf6d7da-e054-43b3-a9a8-7b2fd4133c39.filesusr.com/ugd/bdf8dc_79f1f9456e164e918c8050944468218d.pdf

Anderson, B. (1991). *Imagined Communities: Reflections on the Origin and Spread of Nationalism*, 2nd edn. London: Verso.

AP Archive (2015). Venezuela joins South America trade bloc [Video]. 21 July. Retrieved from www.youtube.com/watch?v=H-v087tdX3k

Arugay, A. A. (2018). When populists perform foreign policy: Duterte and the Asia-Pacific Regional Order. *SWP Working Papers*, 4. Retrieved from www

.swp-berlin.org/fileadmin/contents/products/projekt_papiere/Arugay_BCAS _Philippines.pdf

Aslanidis, P. (2016). Is populism an ideology? A refutation and a new perspective. *Political Studies*, 64(IS), 88–104.

Barr, R. R. (2009). Populists, outsiders and anti-establishment politics. *Party Politics*, 15(1), 29–48.

Bastenier, M. A. (2012) Caribbean Mercosur: Venezuela's entry to the trade bloc highlights pivotal role Chavez plays in the region's politics. *El Pais*, 9 August. Retrieved from https://english.elpais.com/elpais/2012/08/09/ inenglish/1344515660_744168.html

Bauerová, H. (2018). Migration policy of the V4 in the context of migration crisis. *Politics in Central Europe*, 14(2), 99–120. https://doi.org/10.2478/ pce-2018-0011

Baviera, A. (2016). President Duterte's foreign policy challenges. *Contemporary Southeast Asia: A Journal of International and Strategic Affairs*, 38(2), 202–8.

Baviera, A. & Pante, M. D. (2019). Philippines-China relations, maritime disputes, and the broader environment. *Philippine Studies: Historical and Ethnographic Viewpoints*, 67(1), 113–20.

Benford, R. D. & Snow, D. A. (2000). Framing processes and social movements: An overview and assessment. *Annual Review of Sociology*, 26, 611–39.

Bilotta, N. (2018). The legacy of post-neoliberal integration in South America: The cases of ALBA and UNASUR. *IAI papers*, 2018 (20).

Bíró-Nagy A. (2017). Illiberal democracy in Hungary: The social background and practical steps of building an illiberal state. In P. Morillas, ed., *Illiberal Democracies in the EU: The Visegrad Group and the Risk of Disintegration*. Barcelona: CIDOB, pp. 31–44.

Bonikowski, B. (2017). Ethno-nationalist populism and the mobilization of collective resentment. *British Journal of Sociology*, 86(S1), 181–213. https://doi.org/10.1111/1468-4446.12325

Bonikowski, B., Halikiopoulou, D., Kaufmann, E., & Rooduijn, M. (2019). Populism and nationalism in a comparative perspective: A scholarly exchange. *Journal of the Association for the Study of Ethnicity and Nationalism*, 25(1), 58–81. https://doi.org/10.1111/nana.12480

Börzel, T. A. & Van Hüllen, V. (2015). *Governance Transfer by Regional Organizations: Patching Together a Global Script*. Basingstoke: Palgrave Macmillan.

Börzel, T. A. & Risse, T. (2019). Global contestations of the liberal order. Section abstract. Sixth Global International Studies Conference, Buenos Aires, 15–17 June.

Börzel, T. A. & Zürn, M. (2021). Contestations of the liberal international order: From liberal multilateralism to postnational liberalism. *International Organization*, 1-24. doi:10.1017/S0020818320000570

Braun, M. (2020). Post-functionalism, identity and the Visegrad Group. *Journal of Common Market Studies*, 58(4), 925–40. https://doi.org/10.1111/jcms.12994

Brown, K. L. (2010). Venezuela joins Mercosur: The impact felt around the Americas. *Law and Business Review of the Americas*, 16(1), 85–94.

Burges, S. W. (2007). Building a global southern coalition: The competing approaches of Brazil's Lula and Venezuela's Chávez. *Third World Quarterly*, 28(7), 1343–58.

Burrier, G. A. (2019). Populists and foreign policy: Evidence from Latin America. In F. A. Stengel, D. B. MacDonald, & D. Nabers, eds, *Populism in World Politics*. Basingstoke: Palgrave Macmillan, pp. 165–94.

Buzogány, A. (2017). Illiberal democracy in Hungary: Authoritarian diffusion or domestic causation? *Democratization*, 24(7), 1307–25. https://doi.org/10.1080/13510347.2017.1328676

Cabada, L. (2018). The Visegrad cooperation in the context of other Central European cooperation formats. *Politics in Central Europe*, 14(2), 165–79. https://doi.org/10.2478/pce-2018-0014

Cabada, L. & Waisová, S. (2018). The Visegrad Group as an ambitious actor of (Central-European) foreign and security policy. *Politics in Central Europe*, 14(2), 9–20. https://doi.org/10.2478/pce-2018-0006

Calayag, K. (2021). Duterte-Biden friendship seen to bloom. *The Manila Times*, 21 January. Retrieved from www.manilatimes.net/2021/01/21/news/top-stories/duterte-biden-friendship-seen-to-bloom/830129/

Calonzo, A. (2019). Xi, Duterte fail to reach agreement on South China Sea issues. *Bloomberg*, 30 August. Retrieved from www.bloomberg.com/news/articles/2019-08-30/xi-duterte-agreed-to-disagree-no-deal-on-exploration-sea-row

Canovan, M. (1999). Trust the people! Populism and the two faces of democracy. *Political Studies*, 47(1), 2–16. https://doi.org/10.1111/1467-9248.00184

Canovan, M. (2002). Taking politics to the people: Populism as the ideology of democracy. In Y. Mény & Y. Surel, eds., *Democracies and the Populist Challenge*. London: Palgrave Macmillan, pp. 25–44.

Carranza, M. E. (2010). Mercosur, the global economic crisis and the new architecture of regionalism in Latin America. FLACSO Working Paper No. 125.

Chávez, H. (2005). Discurso: Clausura de la III Cumbre de los Pueblos de America. *Cadena Nacional de Radio y Television*, 4 November. Retrieved from www.nodal.am/2015/11/a-diez-anos-del-no-al-alca-discruso-com pleto-de-hugo-chavez-en-la-contra-cumbre/

Chávez, H. (2013). *Mensaje*. I Cumbre de la Comunidad de Estados Latinoamericanos y Caribeños (CELAC), 28 January. Retrieved from www .ctmargentina.org/sitio-archivo/pdfs/CumbreCELACMensajeHugoChavez .pdf.

Chávez, H. & Castro, F. (2004). Declaración Conjunta Venezuela–Cuba. I Cumbre ALBA, La Habana. *ALBA Portal*, 14 December. Retrieved from http://albatcp.cubaminrex.cu/page/i-cumbre-la-habana-14-de-diciembre-2004.

Checkel, J. T. & Katzenstein, P. J. (2009). *The Politicization of European Identities*. Cambridge: Cambridge University Press.

Chodor, T. & McCarthy-Jones, A. (2013). Post-liberal regionalism in Latin America and the influence of Hugo Chávez. *Journal of Iberian and Latin American Research*, 19(2), 211–23. https://doi.org/10.1080/13260219.2013.853353

Chongkittavorn, K. (2016). ASEAN: Duterte's China move. *Reporting Asean*, 16 November. Retrieved from https://www.reportingasean.net/asean-dutertes-china-move/

Christensen, S. F. (2007). The influence of nationalism in Mercosur and in South America – can the regional integration project survive? *Revista Brasileira de Política Internacional*, 50(1), 139–58. http://dx.doi.org/10.1590/S0034-73292007000100008

Chryssogelos, A. (2010). Undermining the West from within: European populists, the US and Russia. *European View*, 9(2), 267–77. https://doi.org/10.1007/s12290-010-0135-1

Chryssogelos, A. (2014). Reaction and adaptation in the longue durée: The far-right, international politics and the state in historical perspective. In R. Saull, A. Anievas, N. Davidson, & A. Fabry, eds, *The Longue Durée of the Far-Right: An International Historical Sociology*. London: Routledge, pp. 85–105.

Chryssogelos, A. (2017). Populism in foreign policy. In *Oxford Research Encyclopedia of Politics*. Oxford: Oxford University Press. https://doi.org/10.1093/acrefore/9780190228637.013.467

Colgan, J. & Keohane, R. (2017). The liberal order is rigged: Fix it now or watch it wither. *Foreign Affairs*, 96(3), 36–44.

Coman, R. & Leconte, C. (2019). Contesting EU authority in the name of European identity: The new clothes of the sovereignty discourse in Central Europe. *Journal of European Integration*, 41(7), 855–70. https://doi.org/10.1080/07036337.2019.1665660

Copelovitch, M. & Pevehouse, J. (2019). International organizations in a new era of populist nationalism. *Review of International Organizations*, 14(2), 169–86. https://doi.org/10.1007/s11558-019-09353-1

Csehi, R. (2019). Neither episodic, nor destined to failure? The endurance of Hungarian populism after 2010. *Democratization*, 26(6), 1011–27. https://doi.org/10.1080/13510347.2019.1590814

Curato, N. (2017). We need to talk about Rody. In N. Curato, ed., *A Duterte Reader: Critical Essays on Rodrigo Duterte's Early Presidency*. Quezon City: Ateneo de Manila University Press, pp. 1–38.

Cusack, A. K. (2019). *Venezuela, ALBA, and the Limits of Postneoliberal Regionalism in Latin America and the Caribbean*. New York: Palgrave Macmillan.

Dabène, O. (2012). Consistency and resilience through cycles of repoliticization. In P. Riggirozzi & D. Tussie, eds, *The Rise of Post-Hegemonic Regionalism*. Dordrecht: Springer, pp. 41–64.

Daily News Hungary (2019). Prime Minister Viktor Orbán met Mart Helme, deputy prime minister and interior minister of Estonia, for talks in Budapest on Monday. 8 July. Retrieved from https://dailynewshungary.com/estonia-deputy-pm-helme-held-talks-in-budapest/

Davies, M. (2018). *Ritual and Region: The Invention of ASEAN*. Cambridge: Cambridge University Press.

De Castro, R. C. (2018). Explaining the Duterte administration's appeasement policy on China: The power of fear. *Asian Affairs: An American Review*, 45 (3–4), 165–91. https://doi.org/10.1080/00927678.2019.1589664

De Castro, R. C. (2019). China's Belt and Road Initiative (BRI) and the Duterte administration's appeasement policy: Examining the connection between the two national strategies. *East Asia*, 36, 205–27. https://doi.org/10.1007/s12140-019-09315-9

De Cleen, B. (2017). Populism and nationalism. In C. Rovira Kaltwasser, P. Ochoa Espejo, & P. Ostiguy, eds, *The Oxford Handbook of Populism*. Oxford: Oxford University Press, pp. 342–362. https://doi.org/10.1093/oxfordhb/9780198803560.013.18

De Cleen, B. & Stavrakakis, Y. (2017). Distinctions and articulations: A discourse theoretical framework for the study of populism and nationalism. *Javnost – The Public*, 24(4), 301–19. https://doi.org/10.1080/13183222.2017.1330083

De Cleen, B., Moffitt, B., Panayotu, P., & Stavrakakis, Y. (2019). The potentials and difficulties of transnational populism: The case of the Democracy in Europe Movement 2025 (DiEM25). *Political Studies*, 68(1), 146–66. https://doi.org/10.1177/0032321719847576

De la Fuente, E. (2011). ALBA: A political tool for Venezuela's foreign policy. *Western Hemisphere Security Analysis Center*, 4. Retrieved from https://digitalcommons.fiu.edu/whemsac/4

De Spiegeleire, S., Skinner, C., & Sweijs, T. (2017). *The Rise of Populist Sovereignism: What It Is, Where It Comes From, and What It Means for International Security and Defense.* The Hague: The Hague Centre for Strategic Studies.

Debre, M. J. & Morgenbesser, L. (2017). Out of the shadows: Autocratic regimes, election observation and legitimation. *Contemporary Politics*, 23 (3), 328–47. https://doi.org/10.1080/13569775.2017.1304318

Dellmuth, L. M., Scholte, J. A., Tallberg, J., & Verhaegen, S. (2019). The elite–citizen gap in international organization legitimacy. Paper presented at the APSA Annual Meeting, Washington, DC, 28 August–1 September.

Destradi, S. & Plagemann, J. (2019). Populism and international relations: (Un) predictability, personalisation, and the reinforcement of existing trends in world politics. *Review of International Studies*, 45(5), 711–30. https://doi.org/10.1017/S0260210519000184

Di Tella, T. S. (1965). Populismo y reforma en América Latina. *Desarrollo Económico*, 4(16), 391–425.

Dodson, M. & Dorraj, M. (2008). Populism and foreign policy in Venezuela and Iran. *Whitehead Journal of Diplomacy and International Relations*, 9, 71–87.

Duterte, R. (2016a). Closing ceremony of the 28th and 29th ASEAN Summits (speech) 9/8/2016. *Youtube*, 8 September [Video]. Retrieved from www.youtube.com/watch?v=TwJBxbtZ6Ds

Duterte, R. (2016b). Departure speech of President Rodrigo Roa Duterte (Sept 5, 2016). *Official Gazette*, 5 September. Retrieved from www.officialgazette.gov.ph/2016/09/05/departure-speech-of-president-rodrigo-roa-duterte-sept-5-2016/

Duterte, R. (2017a). Remarks of President Rodrigo Roa Duterte at the Opening Ceremony of the 30th ASEAN Summit, PICC, Manila. *ASEAN*, 29 April. Retrieved from https://asean.org/remarks-president-rodrigo-roa-duterte-opening-ceremony-30th-asean-summit-picc-manila-philippines-29-april-2017/

Duterte, R. (2017b). Speech of President Duterte during ASEAN 2017 opening ceremony. *Business World*, 13 November. Retrieved from www.bworldonline.com/full-transcript-speech-pres-duterte-asean-2017-opening-ceremony/

Duterte, R. (2017c). Rodrigo Roa Duterte, Second State of the Nation Address, July 24, 2017. *Official Gazette*, 24 July. Retrieved from www.officialgazette.gov.ph/2017/07/24/rodrigo-roa-duterte-second-state-of-the-nation-address-july-24-2017/

Duterte, R. (2018). Rodrigo Roa Duterte, Third State of the Nation Address, July 23, 2018. *Official Gazette*, 23 July. Retrieved from www.officialgazette.gov.ph/2018/07/23/rodrigo-roa-duterte-third-state-of-the-nation-address-july-23-2018/

Duterte, R. (2019a). Intervention of President Rodrigo Roa Duterte during the 34th ASEAN Summit, Bangkok. 22 June. Retrieved from https://pcoo.gov .ph/wp-content/uploads/2019/06/20190622-INTERVENTION-OF-PRESIDENT-RODRIGO-ROA-DUTERTE-DURING-THE-34TH-ASEAN-SUMMIT-PLENARY.pdf

Duterte, R. (2019b). Rodrigo Roa Duterte, Fourth State of the Nation Address. *Official Gazette*, 22 July. Retrieved from www.officialgazette.gov.ph/2019/ 07/22/rodrigo-roa-duterte-fourth-state-of-the-nation-address-july-22-2019/

East Asia Forum (2017). Manila's pivot to pragmatism on the South China Sea. 14 August. Retrieved from www.eastasiaforum.org/2017/08/14/manilas-pivot-to-pragmatism-on-the-south-china-sea/

El 19 (2015). Chávez, el líder que más hizo por la integración de América Latina. 5 March. Retrieved from www.el19digital.com/articulos/ver/ titulo:26805-chavez-el-lider-que-mas-hizo-por-la-integracion-de-america-latina

Entman, R. M. (1993). Framing: Toward clarification of a fractured paradigm. *Journal of Communication*, 43(4), 51–8.

Enyedi, Z. (2016). Paternalist populism and illiberal elitism in Central Europe. *Journal of Political Ideologies*, 21(1), 9–25. https://doi.org/10.1080/ 13569317.2016.1105402

ERIA (Economic Research Institute for ASEAN and East Asia) (2017). Empower the ASEAN peoples, President Duterte tells govts. 23 October. Retrieved from www.eria.org/database-and-programmes/empower-the-asean-peoples-president-duterte-tells-govts/

Europa Press (2011). Chávez expresa su deseo de que la CELAC sustituya 'en los próximos años' a la OEA. *Notimérica*, 2 December. Retrieved from www .notimerica.com/politica/noticia-celac-chavez-expresa-deseo-celac-susti tuya-proximos-anos-oea-20111202041336.html

Franco, F. (2012). Nosso problema nao e a Venezuela, mas Chavez dentro do Mercosul. Interview. *Estadão*, 5 August. Retrieved from https://internacio nal.estadao.com.br/noticias/geral,nosso-problema-nao-e-a-venezuela-mas-chavez-dentro-do-mercosul-imp-,911400

Fougère, M. & Barthold, C. (2020). Onwards to the new political frontier: Macron's electoral populism. *Organization*, 27(3), 419–30. https://doi.org/ 10.1177/1350508420910567

Galston, W. (2018). The populist challenge to liberal democracy. *Journal of Democracy*, 29(2), 5–19. https://doi.org/10.1353/jod.2018.0020

Garcia, N. A. (2012). 21st century regionalism in South America: UNASUR and the search for development alternatives. *eSharp* 18, 64–85.

Gardini, G. L. (2011). MERCOSUR: What you see is not (always) what you get. *European Law Journal*, 17(5), 683–700. https://doi.org/10.1111/j.1468-0386.2011.00573.x

Gardner, S. (2009). Chavez rhetoric stokes Honduras crisis before talks. *Reuters*, 17 July. Retrieved from www.reuters.com/article/idINIndia-41133020090717

Gita, R. A. (2016). Duterte confirms showing photo of killed Moros before Asean delegates. *Sun Star Philippines*, 9 September. Retrieved from www.sunstar.com.ph/article/97202

Goffman, E. (1974). *Frame Analysis: An Essay on the Organization of Experience*. Boston, MA: Northeastern University Press.

Gotkowska, J. (2017). The CSDP's renaissance: Challenges and opportunities for the eastern flank. OSW Commentary No. 243, 28 October. Retrieved from www.osw.waw.pl/sites/default/files/commentary_243.pdf

Gouvea, R. & Montoya, M. (2014). Mercosur after Chavez. *Thunderbird International Business Review*, 56(6),563–75. https://doi-org.ezproxy.ub.gu.se/10.1002/tie.21650

Guevara, A. (2005). *Chávez, Venezuela and the New Latin America: An Interview with Hugo Chávez*. Melbourne: Ocean Press.

Gürcan, E. C. (2019). *Multipolarization, South–South Cooperation, and the Rise of Post-Hegemonic Governance*. London & New York: Routledge.

Gurzu, A., De la Baume, M., Bayer, L., & Paun, C. (2019). Ursula von der Leyen's rejection headache: Romanian and Hungarian nominees fall foul of Parliament committee. *Politico*, 29 September. Retrieved from www.politico.eu/article/rovana-plumb-laszlo-trocsanyi-meps-reject-romania-hungary-nominees-for-european-commission/

Hadiz, V. R. & Chryssogelos, A. (2017). Populism in world politics: A comparative cross-regional perspective. *International Political Science Review*, 38(4), 399–411. https://doi.org/10.1177/0192512117693908

Hafner-Burton, E. M., Mansfield, E. D., & Pevehouse, J. (2015). Human rights institutions, sovereignty costs and democratization. *British Journal of Political Science*, 45(1), 1–27. https://doi.org/10.1017/S0007123413000240

Halikiopoulou, D., Nanou, K., & Vasilopoulou, S. (2012). The paradox of nationalism: The common denominator of radical right and radical left Euroscepticism. *European Journal of Political Research*, 51(4), 504–39. https://doi.org/10.1111/j.1475-6765.2011.02050.x

Hameleers, M., Bos, L., & De Vreese, C. (2018). Framing blame: Towards a better understanding of the effects of populist communication on populist party preferences. *Journal of Elections, Public Opinion and Parties*, 28(3), 380–98. https://doi.org/10.1080/17457289.2017.1407326

Hawkins, K. A. (2016). Responding to radical populism: Chavismo in Venezuela. *Democratization*, 23(2), 242–62. https://doi.org/10.1080/13510347.2015.1058783

Herrmann, R. K., Risse, T., & Brewer, M. B. (2004). *Transnational Identities: Becoming European in the EU*. Lanham, MD: Rowman & Littlefield.

Heydarian, R. J. (2017). Tragedy of small power politics: Duterte and the shifting sands of Philippine foreign policy. *Asian Security*, 13(3), 220–36. https://doi.org/10.1080/14799855.2017.1354569

Heydarian, R. J. (2018). *The Rise of Duterte: A Populist Revolt Against Elite Democracy*. Basingstoke: Palgrave Macmillan.

Higgott, R. & Proud, V. (2017). *Populist-Nationalism and Foreign Policy: Cultural Diplomacy, International Interaction and Resilience*. Stuttgart: IFA (Institut für Auslandsbeziehungen).

Hokovský, R. (2017). The role of Visegrad Group in the EU: The view from the inside. In L. Tungul, ed., *The Czech Centre-Right Solutions to the Political Challenges of 2018*. Prague: Wilfried Mertens Centre for European Studies & TOPAZ, pp. 51–5.

Holliday, S. J. (2019). Populism, the international and methodological nationalism: Global order and the Iran–Israel nexus. *Political Studies*, 68(1), 3–19. https://doi.org/10.1177/0032321718817476

Hooghe, L., Lenz, T., & Marks, G. (2019). Contested world order: The delegitimation of international governance. *Review of International Organizations*, 14(4), 731–43. https://doi.org/10.1007/s11558-018-9334-3

Hooghe, L. & Marks, G. (2009). A postfunctionalist theory of European integration: From permissive consensus to constraining dissensus. *British Journal of Political Science*, 39(1), 1–23. https://doi.org/10.1017/S0007123408000409

Huang, E. & Steger, I. (2016). 'I am Chinese': Rodrigo Duterte explained the Philippines' shift in the South China Sea to China's CCTV. *Quartz*, 19 October. Retrieved from https://qz.com/813171/i-am-chinese-president-rodrigo-duterte-explained-the-philippines-shift-in-the-south-china-sea-to-chinas-cctv/

Hungary Journal (2018). Orban: Europe is the home of nations. 23 October. Retrieved from https://thehungaryjournal.com/2018/10/23/orban-europe-is-the-home-of-nations/

Hungary Today (2018). Orbán: Government serves nation 'but our place is in Europe'. 18 May. Retrieved from https://hungarytoday.hu/orban-government-serves-nation-but-our-place-is-in-europe/

Huong, L. T. (2018). China's dual strategy of coercion and inducement towards ASEAN. *The Pacific Review*, 32(1), 20–36. https://doi.org/10.1080/09512748.2017.1417325

Ikenberry, G. J. (2011). *Liberal Leviathan: The Origins, Crisis, and Transformation of the American World Order*. Princeton, NJ: Princeton University Press.

Ikenberry, G. J. (2018a). The end of the liberal international order? *International Affairs*, 94(1), 7–23. https://doi.org/10.1093/ia/iix241

Ikenberry, G. J. (2018b). Why the liberal world order will survive. *Ethics & International Affairs*, 32(1), 17–29. https://doi.org/10.1017/S0892679418000072

Ileto, R. C. (1993). The 'Unfinished Revolution' in Philippine political discourse. *Southeast Asian Studies*, 31(1), 62–82.

Inotai, E. (2019). What Orbán wants: Inside Hungary's EU strategy. *Reporting Democracy*, 20 May. Retrieved from https://balkaninsight.com/2019/05/20/what-orban-wants-inside-hungarys-eu-strategy/

Jácome, F. (2012). Alcances y desafíos del liderazgo venezolano en América Latin. In J. Altmann Borbón, ed., *América Latina: Caminos de la integración regional*. San José: FLASCO, pp. 71–88.

Jenne, E., & Mudde, C. (2012). Hungary's illiberal turn: Can outsiders help? *Journal of Democracy*, 23(3), 147–55. https://doi.org/10.1353/jod.2012.0057

Jennings, R. (2017). Duterte to ASEAN leaders: Be 'resolute in realizing a drug-free ASEAN'. *VOA News*, 29 April. Retrieved from www.voanews.com/east-asia-pacific/duterte-asean-leaders-be-resolute-realizing-drug-free-asean

Johnston, A. I. (2008). *Social States: China in International Institutions, 1980–2000*. Princeton, NJ: Princeton University Press.

Jozwiak, V. (2016). The Visegrad Group from Hungary's perspective. PISM Bulletin No. 86. Retrieved from www.ceeol.com/search/gray-literature-detail?id=591125

Jozwiak, V. (2017). Hungarian presidency of the Visegrad Group. PISM Bulletin No. 77. Retrieved from www.ceeol.com/search/gray-literature-detail?id=578662

Juego, B. (2017). The Philippines 2017: Duterte-led authoritarian populism and its liberal-democratic roots. *Asia Maior*, 28, 129–63.

Jupille, J., Jolliff, B., & Wojcik, S. (2013). Regionalism in the world polity. Paper prepared for the Annual Convention of the International Studies Association, San Francisco, CA, 3–6 April. http://dx.doi.org/10.2139/ssrn.2242500

Kagan, R. (2017). The twilight of the liberal world order. In M. E. O'Hanlon, ed., *Brookings Big Ideas for America*. Washington, DC: The Brookings Institution, pp. 267–74.

Katigbak, J. J. P. (2017). RCEP and the future of Asian free trade agreements: A Philippine perspective. *CIRSS Commentaries*, 4(2), 1–3.

Kenny, P. (2018). *Populism in Southeast Asia.* Cambridge: Cambridge University Press.

Kent, A. (2002). China's international socialization: The role of international organizations. *Global Governance*, 8(3), 343–64.

Kneuer, M., Demmelhuber, T., Peresson, R., & Zumbrägel, T. (2019). Playing the regional card: Why and how authoritarian gravity centres exploit regional organisations. *Third World Quarterly*, 40(3), 451–70.

Kořan, M. (2012). The Visegrad Group on the threshold of its third decade: A Central European hub? In Z. Šabič & P. Drulák, eds, *Regional and International Relations of Central Europe.* London: Palgrave Macmillan, pp. 201–18.

Kovács, Z. (2019). PM Orbán: We can only support EU leaders who respect Central Europe. *About Hungary*, 14 June. Retrieved from http://abouthungary .hu/blog/pm-orban-we-can-only-support-eu-leaders-who-respect-central-europe/

Krekó, P. & Enyedi, Z. (2018). Explaining Eastern Europe: Orbán's laboratory of illiberalism. *Journal of Democracy*, 29(3), 39–51.

Kreuder-Sonnen, C. (2018) An authoritarian turn in Europe and European studies? *Journal of European Public Policy*, 25(3), 452–64. https://doi.org/ 10.1080/13501763.2017.1411383

Kreuder-Sonnen, C. & Rittberger, B. (2020). The LIO's share: How the liberal international order contributes to its own legitimacy crisis. CES Open Forum Series 39. Retrieved from https://ces.fas.harvard.edu/uploads/files/Open-Forum-Papers/Working-Paper-Kreuder-Sonnen-April-2020-FINAL.pdf

Kupchan, C. A. (2012). *No One's World: The West, the Rising Rest, and the Coming Global Turn.* Oxford: Oxford University Press.

Kurlantzick, J. (2018). Southeast Asia's populism is different but also dangerous. *Council on Foreign Relations*, 1 November. Retrieved from www.cfr .org/in-brief/southeast-asias-populism-different-also-dangerous

Lacorte, R. (2016). Duterte to Obama: Don't lecture me on rights, PH not a US colony. *Philippine Daily Inquirer*, 5 September. Retrieved from https://glo balnation.inquirer.net/143883/duterte-to-obama-dont-lecture-me-on-rights-ph-not-a-us-colony

Laclau, E. (2005). *On Populist Reason.* London: Verso.

Laclau, E. & Mouffe, C. (2001). *Hegemony and Socialist Strategy: Towards a Radical Democratic Politics.* London: Verso.

Layne, C. (2012). This time it's real: The end of unipolarity and the Pax Americana. *International Studies Quarterly*, 56(1), 203–13. https://doi.org/ 10.2307/41409832

Legler, T. (2010a). El perfil del multilateralismo latinoamericano. *Foreign Affairs Latinoamérica*, 10(3), 2–5.

Legler, T. (2010b). Gobernanza regional: El vínculo multilateral. *Foreign Affairs Latinoamérica*, 10(3), 18–23.

Legler, T. (2013). Post-hegemonic regionalism and sovereignty in Latin America: Optimists, skeptics, and an emerging research agenda. *Contexto Internacional*, 35(2), 325–52.

Lenz, T. (2018). Frame diffusion and institutional choice in regional economic cooperation. *International Theory*, 10(1), 31–70. https://doi.org/10.1017/S1752971917000136

Li, X. (2012). Understanding China's behavioral change in the WTO dispute settlement system. *Asian Survey*, 52(6), 1111–37.

Looney, R. E. (2018). *Handbook of International Trade Agreements: Country, Regional and Global Approaches*. London: Routledge.

Magcamit, M. I. (2018). The Duterte Doctrine: A neoclassical realist guide to understanding Rodrigo Duterte's foreign policy and strategic behavior in the Asia-Pacific. APPFI Working Paper 2018-01.

Mair, P. (2009). Representative versus responsible government. Max Planck Institute for the Study of Societies Working Paper 2009/08.

Malamud, C. (2006). Venezuela's withdrawal from the Andean Community of Nations and the consequences for regional integration (Part I). *Area: Latin America*, 54, 1–7.

Manalo, E. A. (2017). The Philippines' chairmanship of ASEAN in 2017. *FSI Insights*, 4(1). Retrieved from www.fsi.gov.ph/the-philippines-chairmanship-of-asean-in-2017/

Mearsheimer, J. (2001). *The Tragedy of Great Power Politics*. New York: W. W. Norton & Co.

Meny, Y. & Surel, Y. (2002). *Democracies and the Populist Challenge*. Basingstoke: Palgrave Macmillan.

Miller-Idriss, C. (2019). The global dimensions of populist nationalism. *The International Spectator*, 54(2), 17–34. https://doi.org/10.1080/03932729.2019.1592870

Miniszterelnok.hu (2019). Hungary belongs to Europe. We are Europe. Website of the Hungarian Government, 7 March. Retrieved from http://www.miniszterelnok.hu/hungary-belongs-to-europe-we-are-europe/

Moffitt, B. (2016). *The Global Rise of Populism: Performance, Political Style, and Representation*. Stanford, CA: Stanford University Press.

Moffitt, B. (2017). Transnational populism? Representative claims, media and the difficulty of constructing a transnational 'people'. *Javnost – The Public*, 24(4), 409–25. https://doi.org/10.1080/13183222.2017.1330086

Moravcsik, A. (1997). Taking preferences seriously: A liberal theory of international politics. *International Organization*, 51(4), 513–53.

Moravcsik, A. (1998). *The Choice for Europe: Social Purpose and State Power from Messina to Maastricht*. Ithaca, NY: Cornell University Press.

Mos, M. (2020). Ambiguity and interpretive politics in the crisis of European values: Evidence from Hungary. *East European Politics*, 36(2), 267–87. https://doi.org/10.1080/21599165.2020.1724965

Mothiane, M. (2016). Sustaining regional integration in South America: The case of Mercosur. Economic Policy Forum, Paper 5. Retrieved from https://economic-policy-forum.org/wp-content/uploads/2016/02/Sustaining-Regional-Integration.pdf

Mudde, C. (2004). The populist zeitgeist. *Government and Opposition*, 39(4), 541–63. https://doi.org/10.1111/j.1477-7053.2004.00135.x

Mudde, C. & Rovira Kaltwasser, C. (2011). Voices of the peoples: Populism in Europe and Latin America compared. Kellogg Institute Working Paper No. 378. https://kellogg.nd.edu/sites/default/files/old_files/documents/378_0.pdf

Mudde, C., & Rovira Kaltwasser, C. (2013). Exclusionary vs. inclusionary populism: Comparing contemporary Europe and Latin America. *Government and Opposition*, 48(2), 147–74. https://doi.org/10.1017/gov.2012.11

Mudde, C., & Rovira Kaltwasser, C. (2017). *Populism: A Very Short Introduction*. Oxford: Oxford University Press.

Müller, J. W. (2016). *What Is Populism?* Philadelphia: University of Pennsylvania Press.

Němec, J. (2007). Prospects for Mercosur after Chávez joining in: Populist threat to the integration bloc? In J. Němec, ed., *Global and Regional Governance: Europe and Beyond*. Prague: University of Economics, pp. 79–88.

Nič, M. (2016). The Visegrád Group in the EU: 2016 as a turning-point? *European View*, 15(2), 281–90. https://doi.org/10.1007/s12290-016-0422-6

NTN24 (2012). Hugo Chávez se pronuncia tras el ingreso de su país al grupo Mercosur. *Youtube* [Video]. Retrieved from www.youtube.com/watch?v=OBGLkWmZBQg

Obydenkova, A. V. & Libman, A. (2019). *Authoritarian Regionalism in the World of International Organizations: Global Perspective and the Eurasian Enigma*. Oxford: Oxford University Press.

Orbán, V. (2012). Speech at the plenary session of the European Parliament. Website of the Hungarian Government, 18 January. Retrieved from https://2010-2014.kormany.hu/en/prime-minister-s-office/the-prime-ministers-speeches/speech-at-the-plenary-session-of-the-european-parliament

Orbán, V. (2013). Prime Minister Orbán's closing speech in the European Parliament. Website of the Hungarian Government, 2 July. Retrieved from https://2010-2014.kormany.hu/en/prime-minister-s-office/the-prime-ministers-speeches/prime-minister-orban-s-closing-speech-in-the-european-parliament

Orbán, V. (2014). Full text of Viktor Orbán's speech at Băile Tuşnad (Tusnádfürdő) of 26 July 2014. *The Budapest Beacon*, 29 July. Retrieved from https://budapestbeacon.com/full-text-of-viktor-orbans-speech-at-baile-tusnad-tusnadfurdo-of-26-july-2014/

Orbán, V. (2015). Viktor Orbán's speech at the 14th Kötcse civil picnic. *Miniszterelnok.hu*, 5 September. Retrieved from http://2010-2015.miniszter elnok.hu/in_english_article/viktor_orban_s_speech_at_the_14th_kotcse_civil _picnic

Orban, V. (2016a). Prime Minister Viktor Orbán's press statement following the meeting of the Visegrad Group, Prague. *Miniszterelnok.hu*, 15 February. Retrieved from http://2010-2015.miniszterelnok.hu/in_english_article/pri me_minister_viktor_orban_s_press_statement_following_the_meetin g_of_the_visegrad_group

Orbán, V. (2016b). Prime Minister Viktor Orbán's State of the Nation Address. *Miniszterelnok.hu*, 28 February. Retrieved from http://www.miniszterelnok .hu/prime-minister-viktor-orbans-state-of-the-nation-address/

Orbán, V. (2017a). Viktor Orbán's reply in the European Parliament. *Miniszterelnok.hu*, 26 April. Retrieved from http://www.miniszterelnok.hu/ viktor-orbans-reply-in-the-european-parliament/

Orbán, V. (2017b). Prime Minister Viktor Orbán's speech in the European Parliament. *About Hungary*, 26 April. Retrieved from http://abouthungary .hu/prime-minister/prime-minister-viktor-orbans-speech-in-the-european-parliament/

Orbán, V. (2017c). Prime Minister Viktor Orbán's 'State of the Nation' Address. *About Hungary*, 10 February. Retrieved from http://abouthungary.hu/ speeches-and-remarks/prime-minister-viktor-orbans-state-of-the-nation-address-full-text-in-english/

Orbán, V. (2017d). Prime Minister Viktor Orbán's speech marking the transfer of the Visegrád Four presidency. *About Hungary*, 19 June. Retrieved from http://abouthungary.hu/speeches-and-remarks/prime-minister-viktor-orbans-speech-marking-the-transfer-of-the-visegrad-four-presidency/

Orbán, V. (2017e). Viktor Orbán's speech at the 28th Bálványos Summer Open University and Student Camp. *About Hungary*, 22 July. Retrieved from http:// abouthungary.hu/speeches-and-remarks/viktor-orbans-speech-at-the-28th-balvanyos-summer-open-university-and-student-camp/

Orbán, V. (2017f). Hungary and the crisis of Europe. *Hungarian Review*, 8(1). Retrieved from http://hungarianreview.com/article/20170124_hungary_and_the _crisis_of_europe

Orbán, V. (2018a). Prime Minister Viktor Orbán's address after swearing the prime-ministerial oath of office. *Visegrad Post*, 10 May. Retrieved from https://visegradpost.com/en/2018/05/12/viktor-orbans-full-speech-for-the-beginning-of-his-fourth-mandate/

Orbán, V. (2018b). Viktor Orbán's speech at the Visegrád Group conference 'The Future of Europe'. *Miniszterelnok.hu*, 26 January. Retrieved from www.miniszterelnok.hu/viktor-orbans-speech-at-the-visegrad-group-conference-the-future-of-europe/

Orbán, V. (2018c). Debate on the situation in Hungary: Statement by Viktor Orbán, Hungarian prime minister. *European Parliament Multimedia Centre*, 11 September [Video]. Retrieved from https://multimedia.europarl.europa.eu/en/debate-on-the-situation-in-hungary-statement-by-viktor-orbn-hungarian-prime-minister-1531_I160027-V_v

Orbán, V. (2018d). Prime Minister Viktor Orbán's speech on the 62nd anniversary of the 1956 Revolution and Freedom Fight. *Visegrad Post*, 23 October. Retrieved from https://visegradpost.com/en/2018/10/24/viktor-orban-confronts-globalism-and-brussels-in-view-of-upcoming-european-parliament-elections-full-speech/

Orbán, V. (2019a). Prime Minister Viktor Orbán's speech at the 12th Congress of the Federation of Christian Intellectuals (KÉSZ). *About Hungary*, 14 September. Retrieved from http://abouthungary.hu/speeches-and-remarks/prime-minister-viktor-orbans-speech-at-the-12th-congress-of-the-federation-of-christian-intellectuals-kesz/

Orbán, V. (2019b). Prime Minister Viktor Orbán's 'State of the Nation' Address. *Visegrad Post*, 10 February. Retrieved from https://visegradpost.com/en/2019/02/11/prime-minister-viktor-orbans-state-of-the-nation-address-full-speech/

Orbán, V. (2019c). Interview given by Prime Minister Viktor Orbán to Hungarian Television after special meetings of the European Council. *Miniszterelnok.hu*, 2 July. Retrieved from www.miniszterelnok.hu/interview-given-by-prime-minister-viktor-orban-to-hungarian-television-after-special-meetings-of-the-european-council/

Orban, V. (2019d). Speeches of the Hungarian and Polish prime ministers on the occasion of the Hungarian holiday of March 15. *Website of the Hungarian Government*, 15 March. Retrieved from https://2015-2019.kormany.hu/en/the-prime-minister/the-prime-minister-s-speeches/orban-viktor-s-ceremonial-speech-on-the-171st-anniversary-of-the-hungarian-revolution-and-freedom-fight-of-1848-49

Orbán, V. (2019e). Prime Minister Viktor Orbán on the Kossuth Radio programme 'Good Morning Hungary'. *About Hungary*, 14 June. Retrieved from http://abouthungary.hu/speeches-and-remarks/prime-minister-viktor-orban-on-the-kossuth-radio-programme-good-morning-hungary/

Orbán, V. (2019f). Prime Minister Viktor Orbán on the Kossuth Radio programme 'Good Morning Hungary'. *Miniszterelnok.hu*, 25 October. Retrieved from www.miniszterelnok.hu/prime-minister-viktor-orban-on-the-kossuth-radio-programme-good-morning-hungary-5/

Orbán, V. (2019g). Viktor Orbáns Interview in der Sendung 'Guten Morgen Ungarn' von Radio Kossuth. *Miniszterelnok.hu*, 8 November. Retrieved from http://www.miniszterelnok.hu/viktor-orbans-interview-in-der-sendung-guten-morgen-ungarn-von-radio-kossuth-14/

Orbán, V. (2019h). Exclusive interview with Prime Minister Viktor Orbán for Hungarian Television. *Miniszterelnok.hu*, 1 August. Retrieved from www.miniszterelnok.hu/exclusive-interview-with-prime-minister-viktor-orban-for-hungarian-television/

Orbán, V. (2019i). Prime Minister Viktor Orbán's press statement at the summit of heads of government from the Visegrád Four and Western Balkan countries. *Miniszterelnok.hu*, 12 September. Retrieved from www.miniszterelnok.hu/prime-minister-viktor-orbans-press-statement-at-the-summit-of-heads-of-government-from-the-visegrad-four-and-western-balkan-countries/

Orbán, V. (2019j). Viktor Orbán's press statement following a meeting of the European Council. *Website of the Hungarian Government*, 21 June. Retrieved from https://2015-2019.kormany.hu/en/the-prime-minister/the-prime-minister-s-speeches/viktor-orban-s-press-statement-following-a-meeting-of-the-european-council

Orbán, V. (2020). Prime Minister Viktor Orbán's 'State of the Nation' Address. *About Hungary*, 16 February. Retrieved from http://abouthungary.hu/speeches-and-remarks/prime-minister-viktor-orbans-state-of-the-nation-address-2/

Orellana, P. D. & Michelsen, N. (2019). Reactionary internationalism: The philosophy of the New Right. *Review of International Studies*, 45(5), 748–67. https://doi.org/10.1017/S0260210519000159

Palanca, E. & Ong, A. (2018). Philippines–China relations: Interplay between domestic politics and globalization. In Y. Santasombat, ed., *The Sociology of Chinese Capitalism in Southeast Asia: Challenges and Prospects*. Basingstoke: Palgrave Macmillan, pp. 93–122. https://doi.org/10.1007/978-981-13-0065-3_5

Paterno, E. I. (2016). Duterte pushes for 'drug-free ASEAN'. *Rappler*, 8 September. Retrieved from www.rappler.com/nation/145613-duterte-pushes-drug-free-asean

Peterson, W. & Maiquez R. R. (2020). 'Yesterday's dreams, tomorrow's promise': Performing a pan-ASEAN archipelagic identity at age 50. In M. C. C. Tan & C. Rajendran, eds, *Performing Southeast Asia: Performance, Politics and the Contemporary*. Basingstoke: Palgrave Macmillan, pp. 35–59.

Plattner, F. M. (2019). Illiberal democracy and the struggle on the right. *Journal of Democracy*, 30(1), 5–19. https://doi.org/10.1353/jod.2019.0000

Prime Minister's Office (2016). Prime Minister Viktor Orbán receives Person of the Year award. *Miniszterelnok.hu*, 7 September. Retrieved from http://www.minis zterelnok.hu/prime-minister-viktor-orban-receives-person-of-the-year-award/

Puzyniak, A. (2018). Hungarian foreign policy after 2010: Selected problems. *Facta Simonidis*, 11(1), 231–42. Retrieved from www.ceeol.com/search/article-detail?id=660748

Quiliconi, C. & Salgado Espinoza, R. (2017). Latin American integration: Regionalism à la carte in a multipolar world? *Colombia Internacional*, 92, 15–41. https://doi.org/10.7440/colombiaint92.2017.01

Ranada, P. (2017). Duterte threatens to slap UN rapporteur if she probes drug war. *Rappler*, 9 November. Retrieved from www.rappler.com/nation/187899-duterte-threat-slap-un-rapporteur-callamard

Rappler (2016). Obama scraps meeting with Duterte. 6 September. Retrieved from www.rappler.com/world/regions/asia-pacific/145322-obama-cancels-meeting-duterte

Riggirozzi, P. (2012). Region, regionness and regionalism in Latin America: Towards a new synthesis. *New Political Economy*, 17(4), 421–43. https://doi.org/10.1080/13563467.2011.603827

Riggirozzi, P. & Tussie, D., eds. (2012). *The Rise of Post-Hegemonic Regionalism: The Case of Latin America*. Dordecht: Springer.

Risse, T. (2016). The diffusion of regionalism. In T. A. Börzel & T. Risse, eds, *The Oxford Handbook of Comparative Regionalism*. Oxford: Oxford University Press, pp. 87-107.

Romero, C. & Mijares, V. (2016). From Chávez to Maduro: Continuity and change in Venezuelan foreign policy. *Contexto internacional*, 38(1), 165–201. https://doi.org/10.1590/S0102-8529.2016380100005

Ross, E. (2017). U.S. and the Philippines: President Rodrigo Duterte's most insulting quotes about America. *Newsweek*, 30 June. Retrieved from www.newsweek.com/philippines-president-rodrigo-duterte-one-year-quotes-630011

Roughneen, S. & Smith, N. (2018). Duterte goes to war with UN as he threatens to throw rights team to the crocodiles. *The Telegraph*, 12 March. Retrieved from www.telegraph.co.uk/news/2018/03/12/duterte-goes-war-un-threatens-throw-rights-team-crocodiles/

Ruiz, J. B. (2006). El MERCOSUR y el ALBA en la estrategia de integración de Venezuela. *Cuadernos Latinoamericanos*, 17(30), 97–119.

Ruiz, J. B. (2012). El Alba: Un nuevo eje de la integración regional. In J. A. Borbón, ed., *América Latina: Caminos de la integración regional*. San José: FLASCO, pp. 89–104.

Ruiz-Dana, A., Goldschagg, P., Claro, E., & Blanco, H. (2007). *Regional integration, trade and conflict in Latin America*. Winnipeg: International Institute for Sustainable Development. Retrieved from www.iisd.org/pdf/2007/tas_rta_latin_america.pdf

Russo, A. & Stoddard, E. (2018). Why do authoritarian leaders do regionalism? Ontological security and Eurasian regional cooperation. *The International Spectator*, 53(3), 20–37. https://doi.org/10.1080/03932729.2018.1488404

Schaller, S. & Carius, A. (2019). *Convenient Truths: Mapping Climate Agendas of Right-Wing Populist Parties in Europe*. Berlin: Adelphi.

Serbin, A. & Pont, A. S. (2017). The foreign policy of the Bolivarian republic of Venezuela: The role and legacy of Hugo Chávez. *Latin American Policy*, 8(2), 232–48. https://doi.org/10.1111/lamp.12122

Sevilla, H. A., Jr. (2018). The Philippines' foreign policy direction: An assessment of the first year of President Duterte. *Journal of South Asian Studies*, 6(3), 165–73. https://doi.org/10.33687/jsas.006.03.2558

Slaughter, A. M. (2017). The return of anarchy? *Journal of International Affairs*, 15 March. Retrieved from https://jia.sipa.columbia.edu/return-anarchy

Söderbaum, F. (2016). *Rethinking Regionalism*. Basingstoke: Palgrave Macmillan.

Stengel, F. (2019). Forget populism! *Global Discourse*, 9(2), 445–51. https://doi.org/10.1332/204378919X15628418445603

Stengel, F., MacDonald, D. B., & Nabers, D. (eds.) (2019). *Populism and World Politics*. Basingstoke: Palgrave Macmillan.

Stuenkel, O. (2016). *Post-Western World: How Emerging Powers Are Remaking Global Order*. Cambridge: Polity Press.

Sutherland, C. (2005). Another nation-building bloc? Integrating nationalist ideology into the EU and ASEAN. *Asia Europe Journal*, 3, 141–57. https://doi.org/10.1007/s10308-005-0141-0

Sylvia, R. D. & Danopoulos, C. P. (2003). The Chávez phenomenon: Political change in Venezuela. *Third World Quarterly*, 24(1), 63–76. https://doi.org/10.1080/713701367

Szijjártó, P. (2018). Hungary's goal and interest is a strong and successful Europe. Website of the Hungary News, 3 June. Retrieved from http://hungarynews.hu/2018/06/03/hungarys-goal-and-interest-is-a-strong-and-successful-europe/

Taggart, P. (2000). *Populism*. Buckingham: Open University Press.

Taggart, P. (2004). Populism and representative politics in contemporary Europe. *Journal of Political Ideologies*, 9(3), 269–88. https://doi.org/10.1080/1356931042000263528

Tallberg, J. & Zürn, M. (2019). The legitimacy and legitimation of international organizations: Introduction and framework. *The Review of International Organizations*, 14(4), 581–606. https://doi.org/10.1007/s11558-018-9330-7

Tay, S. S. C. (2017). Imperatives for a new ASEAN leadership: Integration, community, and balance. In A. Baviera & L. Maramis, eds, *Building ASEAN Community: Political-Security and Socio-Cultural Reflections.* Jakarta: Economic Research Institute for ASEAN and East Asia (ERIA), pp. 48–66.

Teehankee, J. C. (2016). Duterte's resurgent nationalism in the Philippines: A discursive institutionalist analysis. *Journal of Current Southeast Asian Affairs*, 35(3), 69–89.

Telesur (2012). Hugo Chávez: Para nosotros el ALBA es la Patria. *Youtube*, 6 February [Video]. Retrieved from www.youtube.com/watch?v=KJOB0w33bm0

Törő, C., Butler, E., & Gruber, K. (2014). Visegrád: The evolving pattern of coordination and partnership after EU enlargement. *Europe–Asia Studies*, 66 (3), 364–93. https://doi.org/10.1080/09668136.2013.855392

Tulmets, E. (2014). *East Central European Foreign Policy Identity in Perspective: Back to Europe and the EU's Neighbourhood.* Basingstoke: Palgrave Macmillan.

Verbeek, B. & Zaslove, A. (2017). Populism and foreign policy. In C. Rovira Kaltwasser, P. Ochoa Espejo, & P. Ostiguy, eds, *The Oxford Handbook of Populism*. Oxford: Oxford University Press, pp. 384–405.

Verbeek, B., & Zaslove, A. (2019). Contested issues surrounding populism in public and academic debates. *The International Spectator*, 54(2), 1–16. https://doi.org/10.1080/03932729.2019.1606513

Wajner, D. F. (2019). Making (Latin) America great again: Lessons from populist foreign policies in the Americas. In F. A. Stengel, D. B. MacDonald, & D. Nabers, eds, *Populism and World Politics*. Basingstoke: Palgrave Macmillan, pp. 195–225.

Wajner, D. F. & Roniger, L. (2019). Transnational identity politics in the Americas: Reshaping 'Nuestramérica' as Chavismo's regional legitimation strategy. *Latin American Research Review*, 54(2), 458–75. https://doi.org/10.25222/larr.43

Weyland, K. (2001). Populism: Clarifying a contested concept. *Comparative Politics*, 34(1), 1–22.

Weyland, K. (2017). Populism: A political-strategic approach. In C. Rovira Kaltwasser, P. Ochoa Espejo, & P. Ostiguy, eds, *The Oxford Handbook of Populism*. Oxford: Oxford University Press, pp. 48–71.

Zakaria, F. (2016). Populism on the march: Why the West is in trouble. *Foreign Affairs*, November/December. Retrieved from www.foreignaffairs.com/art icles/united-states/2016-10-17/populism-march

Zeeman, J. (2019). Populism beyond the nation. In F. A. Stengel, D. B. MacDonald, & D. Nabers, eds, *Populism and World Politics*. Basingstoke: Palgrave Macmillan, pp. 25–53.

Zgut E. & Csehi R. (2019). Orbán's peacock dance. *Aspen Review*, 77–82. Retrieved from www.aspen.review/article/2019/orbans-peacock-dance/

Zürn, M. (2004). Global governance and legitimacy problems. *Government and Opposition*, 39(2), 260–87. https://doi.org/10.1111/j.1477-7053.2004.00123.x

Zürn, M. (2018). *A Theory of Global Governance: Authority, Legitimation and Contestation*. Oxford: Oxford University Press.

Acknowledgements

This Element was written within the framework of a four-year research project entitled 'Regional Cooperation and the Transformation of National Sovereignty' (TRANSFORM), funded by the Swedish Research Council (grant no. 2018–03909), which explores the effects of different understandings of national sovereignty on regional cooperation. Although our original project design was geared towards some carefully selected policy fields in Africa and Southeast Asia (health and water management), we soon discovered that our theoretical framework helped us make sense of why populist leaders engaged in international and regional cooperation, as well as broader questions surrounding the current status and future of the Liberal International Order.

Earlier versions of the Element were presented at the Gothenburg Centre of Globalization and Development workshop '(De)globalization and Development in the New Age of Populisms', Gothenburg, 14–15 November 2019; the Giessen Graduate Centre for Social Sciences, Business, Economics and Law Annual Conference 'Beyond Western Liberalism', Giessen, 2–3 December 2019; the workshop 'Regionalism, International Organizations and Global Challenges in a Fragmented World', Barcelona, 17–18 February 2020; and the workshop of the research project 'Legitimacy in Global Governance', Gothenburg, 4–5 March 2020. We wish to thank the participants at those events for their constructive comments. We also profited from comments on earlier versions by Sandra Destradi, Nicolás Acosta García, Anna-Lena Kirch, and Daniel F. Wajner. We deeply appreciated the input and support from the series editors, Jon Pevehouse and Tanja A. Börzel, as well as an anonymous reviewer. Finally, we are grateful for language editing by John Carville and Marisa Irawan, as well as research assistance by Christopher Lam Cham Kee and Christina de Paris.

About the Authors

Fredrik Söderbaum is Professor of Peace and Development Research at the School of Global Studies, University of Gothenburg, and a Senior Associate Research Fellow at the United Nations University–Comparative Regional Integration Studies (UNU-CRIS), Bruges, Belgium. Söderbaum has published extensively in the fields of comparative regionalism, global and regional governance, development research, and African politics. Recent books include *Rethinking Regionalism* (Macmillan, 2016) and *Intersecting Interregionalism: Regions, Global Governance and the EU* (Springer, 2014).

Kilian Spandler is a researcher at the School of Global Studies, University of Gothenburg. His work explores the conditions of global and regional governance, both historically and against the background of current trends like the rise of populism and the emergence of a post-Western world. He has extensive expertise in Southeast Asian regionalism and is the author of *Regional Organizations in International Society: ASEAN, the EU and the Politics of Normative Arguing* (Palgrave, 2018).

Agnese Pacciardi is an MA student in international security studies at the Sant'Anna School of Advanced Studies in Pisa and the University of Trento, and a research assistant in the research project on Regional Cooperation and the Transformation of National Sovereignty (TRANSFORM) at the School of Global Studies, University of Gothenburg.

Contact details:
Fredrik Söderbaum
University of Gothenburg, School of Global Studies, POB 700, 405 30
    Gothenburg, Sweden
Email: fredrik.soderbaum@gu.se

Cambridge Elements $\equiv$

International Relations

Series Editors

Jon C. W. Pevehouse
University of Wisconsin-Madison

Jon C. W. Pevehouse is the Vilas Distinguished Achievement Professor of Political Science at the University of Wisconsin-Madison. He has published numerous books and articles in IR in the fields of international political economy, international organizations, foreign policy analysis, and political methodology. He is a former editor of the leading IR field journal, *International Organization.*

Tanja A. Börzel
Freie Universität Berlin

Tanja A. Börzel is Professor of Political Science and holds the Chair for European Integration at the Otto-Suhr-Institute for Political Science, Freie Universität Berlin. She holds a PhD from the European University Institute, Florence, Italy. She is coordinator of the Research College 'The Transformative Power of Europe', as well as the FP7-Collaborative Project 'Maximizing the Enlargement Capacity of the European Union', and the H2020 Collaborative Project 'The EU and Eastern Partnership Countries: An Inside-Out Analysis and Strategic Assessment'. She directs the Jean Monnet Center of Excellence 'Europe and its Citizens'.

Edward D. Mansfield
University of Pennsylvania

Edward D. Mansfield is Hum Rosen Professor of Political Science, University of Pennsylvania. He has published well over 100 books and articles in the areas of international political economy, international security, and international organizations. He is Director of the Christopher H. Browne Center for International Politics at the University of Pennsylvania and former program co-chair of the American Political Science Association.

Associate Editors

Jeffrey T. Checkel *European University Institute*
Miles Kahler *American University*

About the Series

Cambridge Elements in International Relations publishes original research on key topics in the field. The series includes manuscripts addressing international security, international political economy, international organizations, and international relations theory. Our objective is to publish cutting edge research that engages crucial topics in each of these issue areas, especially multi-method research that may yield longer studies than leading journals in the field will accommodate.

Cambridge Elements ☰

International Relations

CPSIA information can be obtained
at www.ICGtesting.com
Printed in the USA
BVHW041018170921
616966BV00013B/1156